HUNTING
MATURE BUCKS

by Larry Weishuhn

Published by

krause
publications

700 E. State Street • Iola, WI 54990-0001

Please call or write for our free catalog of outdoor publications. Our toll-free number to place an order or obtain a free catalog is 800-258-0929 or please use our regular business telephone 715-445-2214 for editorial comment and further information.

Library of Congress Catalog Number: 94-73648
ISBN: 0-87341-337-7
Printed in the United States of America

Dedication

To Mary Anne, my wife and companion, for her eternal patience and understanding while I was afield pursuing mature white-tailed bucks. To my daughters, Theresa and Elizabeth, who have at times been hunting partners and always have seemed to know when to be impressed with the deer I bagged.

About the Author

Larry L. Weishuhn brings to whitetail hunting a level of practical and professional experience which few outdoor writers can equal. He has hunted mature whitetails for nearly 40 years, and has worked more than 25 years as a wildlife biologist, specializing in producing mature white-tailed deer.

An author of over 1,000 magazine articles, Weishuhn is on staff with *Deer & Deer Hunting* and other national publications. In addition to this volume, his first book, *Pear Flat Philosophies*, was published in 1994. He is working on several others. He has contributed to several books on hunting and deer biology. He also has scripted, directed and appeared in numerous award-winning outdoor videos and television shows.

Table of Contents

Introduction

Profile of a lifelong deer hunter

From the time I was a youngster growing up in rural Texas, I have been an ardent admirer of white-tailed deer. I grew up listening to tales told by my father of deer and deer hunting. I ravenously read everything I could find about hunting and deer.

Rather than memorize dates of history and study my school books, I memorized rifle ballistic tables and the life histories of game animals. I could quote chapter and verse from several deer hunting books.

When not doing chores or required to be in school, I was "exploring" the woodland pastures behind our country home. My greatest discoveries were shed antlers, deer skulls and spent shells my dad and his friends had shot at whitetails.

After learning how to respect and properly handle a gun I spent many hours each year hunting squirrels and rabbits, even before I was allowed to shoot at a deer. Around our part of rural Texas, hunting was not only a pastime, but a way of life, and one I grew to love and respect.

I have hunted whitetails longer than I can remember. According to my mother, my dad started taking me hunting while I was still in diapers. Some of my fondest early memories are of listening to hunting tales told around the campfire, cleaning deer rifles that really did not need cleaning, and spending time in hunting camp with my mom, dad and brother -- our entire family hunted deer. As a youngster, when not in the deer woods, I dreamed of hunting whitetails and of the day I would take my first eight point buck. How I longed for that day!

My first deer rifle was a .22 rimfire Remington single-shot -- legal back then. I never fired a shot with it at a deer, although I dearly wanted to. During those early years of my hunting, whitetails were scarce. Not until I reached my teens did the deer population in our area start increasing.

From the .22 I graduated to a single-barrel 12-gauge shotgun, which had belonged to my maternal grandfather. With that I took my first white-tailed buck.

To me, that still is the best and most important deer I have ever taken. Visitors to my office view the mount of the spike a bit differently than I do; most do not see it as being the grand deer that it really is. At the point of taking my first deer I became a real deer hunter. Taking that buck only fueled my love of hunting.

My dream of owning a real deer rifle, .30-30 Winchester in a Savage Model 340 bolt action rifle, was realized a couple years after

I took my first deer. I purchased the gun with money earned by hauling hay for my uncles and neighbors. I hunted with that rifle -- topped with an old Weaver K4 scope -- for numerous years, and thankfully still own it. Since then there have been a variety of rifles, muzzleloaders, handguns and even bows, as well as a variety of deer hunts.

With my interest in white-tailed deer and hunting, earning a degree in wildlife science from Texas A & M University seemed like the natural thing to do. In spite of hating school I finally graduated and was fortunate to land a job in the wildlife management field, even before I graduated from college. My interest in whitetails, guns, hunting and managing deer herds for quality animals has never waned. Thank God, there are others who share those same interests, and those numbers are growing!

Focusing on mature whitetails

Big racked white-tailed bucks have fascinated hunters for many years. Our current generation is no exception. If anything, today's hunters, are even more conscious of and interested in the size of racks produced by whitetails than any other generation of hunters. All this interest in producing quality deer has served to promote a management strategy that produces a healthy deer herd and habitat.

Managing deer herds to increase the size of their bodies and antlers requires, in part, the improvement of the overall wildlife habitat. Non-game species thus benefit just as much -- and often much more -- from this type of management as do the targeted species. Perhaps even more important is the fact that the habitat itself benefits.

Several factors influence the size of a buck and the antlers he develops each ensuing year of his life. Age certainly is a major contributing factor. Until a buck reaches three years of age the bones of his skeletal system are still growing. Most of his nutritional intake is used primarily for bone and body development. Those needs always take precedence over those of antler development. Not until all the buck's bones are fully developed will excess nutrients be channeled into antler development. For this reason the best antlers normally are produced by mature bucks.

Some say wisdom comes with age. If that be true, there is good reason why mature bucks (those four years of age and older) are the most difficult to take -- yet the most fun to hunt. Therein comes a most enjoyable challenge. Let us hope future generations will be able to experience the great deer hunting we have had during this latter quarter of the twentieth century.

The lessons of experience

Most of the research, information and stories presented in this volume are based on personal experience. My long-standing love affair with mature white-tailed bucks has been a passionate one. Through those years I have learned much about white-tailed deer. Some of what was learned has long since been forgotten, and much more remains to be learned about whitetails, management and hunting.

I make no claims of having all the answers. If I did, I would be a much better hunter and wildlife biologist than I am. But I was fortunate to enter the scene when hunters and property owners were just beginning to show interest in mature bucks and quality deer herds. I have had the opportunity to be involved with various whitetail research projects and many deer management programs. I also have had the opportunity to hunt some of the finest whitetail country in all of North America, from the edge of Canada's tundra, well into Mexico's arid brushlands.

I write this book about hunting mature white-tailed bucks for numerous reasons. One of those reasons is to share some of my experiences with you the reader. Hopefully those adventures and misadventures will help you learn about mature white-tailed bucks. Hopefully, too, revealing my transgressions in the deer woods will prevent you from making those same mistakes (and if nothing else, they may entertain you).

But when you get right down to it, the best lessons are learned by experience. So after you have faced and been bested by a mature buck, you will reflect fondly on what I have written. You then will know you are not alone in having been made a fool by a majestic white-tailed deer. But remember, regardless of whether you win, or the mature buck wins, there is no finer outdoor challenge than hunting the mature white-tailed buck!

Chapter 1

The Road to Maturity

The saga of Yellow Four

The buck fawn followed closely at his mother's heels. The spots of his first four months were barely distinguishable with the coming of his first winter coat. The bumps on either side of the top part of his head were starting to grow into full-fledged pedicels. Though simply buttons, both the pedicels itched as his first antlers developed. To scratch the itch he rubbed the buttons against his flanks.

Unnoticed by the little buck and the doe that was leading him, I watched from a distance through my 10-power binocular. I knew the young buck well. I had caught him when he was much smaller and attached a small yellow tag to his ear. Through the next several years I would learn much, not only about "Yellow Four," but also about his kind.

I observed the young buck several times that deer season. By the time November arrived he had two short polished spikes, almost an inch long, protruding from his pedicels. During the early fall I occasionally saw this buck feeding in a food plot with several does and other young bucks his age. By the time the rut began, I regularly saw him feeding in the field by himself, or occasionally with other deer his own age. I surmised that when the doe started coming into estrus, the young buck had been weaned and was now forced to make it on his own.

On the last day of the hunting season the tagged buck appeared in a green field with an older buck, one with a massive five point rack. When my hunter squeezed the trigger on the older buck, the young buck nearly turned inside out to get out of the field.

Several days passed before I again saw the young buck. He had taken up residence right across from my hunting camp. There he spent much of the rest of his first year.

The following spring and summer I occasionally saw the tagged buck, his antlers now developing into a nice six point rack. He and several other "fuzzy horned" bucks had formed a young bachelor herd.

The road to maturity starts with birth, and a doe that provides both care and sustenance. Fawns learn survival from the doe.

Throughout this first year he grew in stature and in "survival wisdom" -- the way of the woods.

With the coming of the second autumn, and the hardening of his antlers, Yellow Four and his compatriots started rubbing their antlers. They remained buddies for the month following antler polishing. However, as their hormone levels increased they became less tolerant of each other and started sparring. In addition, younger bucks watched and learned as older bucks rubbed their antlers and made scrape. They followed suit, but visited scrapes only when there were no other bucks around.

During the hunting season several of the tagged buck's summer companions were shot by hunters as part of the ranch's quality management plan. He was present during several of those occasions. By the end of the hunting season he had learned all about hunting, and was starting to learn how to evade hunters.

For the next two years I watched Yellow Four grow into a truly fine buck. At two and a half years of age he sported a beautiful eight point rack, its main beams stretching just beyond his forward pointing ears.

As the fall breeding season approached, his neck started swelling from the hours of rubbing saplings and fighting shrubs in mock battles. He grew irritable, no longer caring for the company of other bucks. When they approached too closely his neck bowed, his ears held tight against his neck in a threatening and menacing manner. If they did not back away he was ready to do full battle.

By the end of his third year and approaching full maturity, Yellow Four had become quite the ladies' man. That fourth fall I saw him many times chasing does, stopping only long enough to challenge any buck that had followed too closely. Several of the hunters on the property mentioned having seen him at many different blind locations. Obviously he was making the rounds. When I saw him at the end of the rut, he looked emaciated and tired. The rut had taken its toll.

That spring I found his sheds, and wondered what his antlers might look like in his fifth autumn. Until the buck turned three years old, he had been easy to find. However during his fourth summer, it seemed as if he had walked up to a still, reflective pond, seen his antlers and resolved to change his ways. That year he developed a massive rack of 10 long points, with a spread well beyond his ears.

During the fifth fall I saw him only occasionally, and then primarily after dark while conducting spotlight game surveys. The buck was easily distinguishable, not only by his small yellow ear tag, but by his large body and impressive antlers. As a four year old he had

Summer can be a time of plenty, or extremely stressful. During the summer bucks frequently form bachelor herds.

developed 12 long tines, including main beams. His tines varied in length from 4 to 12 inches on massive main beams which easily had a 20-inch outside spread.

The hunters on the ranch never saw the buck that fall. I spotted him only twice at a waterhole during the middle of the day while the hunters were in camp for lunch, and a couple of times as he ran across the road late at night. I finally got a good look at him two weeks after the deer season had closed. Rather than appearing emaciated as he had been at the end of his third rutting season, he looked to be in excellent condition.

The next spring, while on a shed antler hunting excursion, I found one of his antlers. It lay in an open area near where I had seen him go to water during the middle of the day, when the deer season had been in full swing.

I did not see the buck again until late August of that year. As a five-year-old, his rack was truly impressive. He displayed 12 long points, with several non-typical points growing from his bases, below the browtines. That fall I started hunting for him, for he was approaching record book proportions.

I spent most of my available hunting time looking for Yellow Four. I tried everything from sitting near food plots, to calling and rattling, to sitting along trails frequented by does. Nothing worked. Finally I glimpsed him during the middle of the day as I was driving from one pasture to another. He ran across the pasture road in front of me, almost as if to taunt me.

After the hunting season I started searching for him at night with a spotlight while conducting other buck research. I could not find him.

During the buck's sixth year I never saw him. Neither could I find him the seventh year, though I tried both night and day. I began to wonder if he had died of natural causes. I would miss the challenge of the old buck and bemoaned his supposed passing.

The following September I was conducting a spotlight game survey on the ranch. We had started an hour after dark, and a little over an hour later we were near the end of our often repeated route. Then, just the edge of the light's reach I spotted what appeared to be the tip of an antler just above the tall brush. Stopping, I studied the spot with my binocular. It was a tine -- and it moved.

Just then the buck stood. He was an absolute monster, a typical 14 point, with extremely long main beams, long tines, massive beams and several points jutting around the base of his antlers. I could hardly believe the size of the buck.

Then I noticed a small yellow tag in his left ear. Without a doubt he was Yellow Four. A moment later he sank into the brush and disappeared.

The lessons of Yellow Four

Yellow Four taught me many things about mature bucks. Most notably, *as bucks mature they change.* They change their habits, and how they act and react. I also learned that *each buck is as individual as you and I.* If you think all deer are created from the same mold and are all the same, that's fine. However, I suspect you face great difficulty in taking mature deer.

If a buck survives to his fourth year -- and, unfortunately, far too many are taken before they have the opportunity to mature -- he has experienced no fewer than four hunting seasons, three of those as a buck with hardened antlers. Chances therefore are excellent that he will have been faced a variety of hunters and hunting tactics. Merely surviving that long, living through several hunting seasons as well as enduring a harsh environment, is quite an accomplishment.

Too often, hunters think of deer only during the hunting season, but that is just a part of the challenge they face. Consider the fighting and rivalry, the lack of eating, and the ragged pace kept during the fall breeding season. And consider the four-legged predators, automobiles, parasites and diseases, extreme winter cold, oppressive summer heat, droughts, floods, poor quality food during the most stressful seasons, and the energy required to complete a set of antlers each fall. All these are stresses faced by deer, especially bucks.

Bucks are ever vigilant, especially after their third summer.

In many ways the stresses deer face are little different from ours. In their case, however, those stresses are a matter of life and death. Yet deer survive.

All bucks are different, not only in their appearance and antler style, but also in their reactions to different situations. Some are destined to develop large antlers and bodies, others are not, regardless of how long they live. Some bucks learn early how to evade hunters and -- obviously -- some do not. Those that do are survivors!

Regardless of their size or where they live, mature bucks are different. Pursuing older bucks the same way you hunt yearlings, or even two-year-old bucks, will greatly reduce your chances of ever taking a mature buck.

The presence of mature bucks in a deer herd does not automatically guarantee a hunter will take a mature deer. Yet, hunters have a great bearing upon the presence or absence of such deer within a population.

As a youngster, the area where I hunted had a growing deer herd. Most of the bucks in our area were fewer than three years of age. True, the deer population was large and growing, and most of the deer there were young. But we hunters primarily would shoot the first bucks we saw. In most instances those were yearling and two-year-old bucks. I was content simply to shoot does and any buck I saw, regardless of their size. Therefore, few mature bucks existed because deer were taken before they were given the opportunity to mature.

The same sort of hunting has existed throughout much of the continent for many years. When hunting in certain areas, where people still practice that type of hunting, I do the same. But I only rarely hunt such areas. However, things are changing. Hunters are becoming increasingly interested in a quality experience and quality deer, measured in terms of large bodies and antlers.

Thankfully, just as there comes maturity in deer there comes maturity in hunters. My reaching that mature stage in deer hunting came quite a few years ago.

The lesson of immaturity

I had hunted for many years and taken quite a few deer. I also had been involved in considerable whitetail research and had, for several years, served as one of the official collectors of animals for research projects. As a result I had "collected" a considerable number of deer. While hunting I had shot a fair number of mature deer, and truly enjoyed the challenge of hunting such bucks, but I was not yet a confirmed hunter of mature bucks.

Then, one cold December afternoon I hunted a ranch just southwest of Abilene, Texas. The property held a fairly high percentage of mature bucks, due to the excellent management program carried on there. I spent most of the afternoon hunting near a deep canyon where previously I had seen a good 10 point with about a 20-inch spread.

Just before dark I noticed movement in the oak brush across the canyon. I was convinced it had to be the big buck I was seeking. The .270 Winchester, Model 700 Remington practically jumped to my shoulder. When the crosshairs settled on the deer's shoulder I squeezed the trigger. He went down immediately. I hurried to where the deer had dropped.

To my disappointment, there at my feet lay a yearling seven point buck, the kind that in three to four years would have been a monster. I nearly cried, wishing I could breathe life back into him and send him on his way. I was extremely aggravated with and disappointed in myself.

An old rancher friend's words spoken earlier that year came back to me: "You'll never kill a big buck if you shoot the first one you see." His words made good sense. And now they haunted me. If I shot the first young buck I saw, I would have no license tag left when a mature buck stepped out.

The man also was correct in another sense. If hunters continue shooting the first buck they see, which is usually a young and often dumb yearling, those bucks are taken out of the herd and never given the opportunity to mature.

As I field-dressed that young North Texas whitetail, I resolved never again to shoot a young buck, and also never again to shoot a buck until I had taken the time to truly evaluate the deer -- not only his antlers, but also his body -- to determine his age. Admittedly, I have on occasion broken that promise, but only when hunting in an area offering no chance of taking a mature buck. However, as stated earlier, I only rarely hunt in such areas.

Hunting mature bucks is not for everyone. Deciding to do so should be a personal decision. To make such a decision often can mean hunting for several days and going home without a buck. And deciding to hunt only -- or primarily -- mature bucks does not mean the bucks you will hunt or take will all be big. As mentioned before, not all bucks are destined to produce huge antlers, even if they've received all the food they wanted and lived to a ripe old age. But even a mature buck with relatively small antlers can be fun to hunt.

Some areas may have a considerable number of mature bucks, and still not produce large-antlered bucks, primarily because of nutrition. I have hunted several coastal areas where this is the case. In those areas an 8 or 10 point buck with a 15-inch outside spread is about as good as they get, regardless of age. Does that mean such bucks are any less challenging to hunt? Certainly not. Big is relative to where you hunt and what is available.

What is a "trophy" buck?

Throughout this book you will seldom, if ever, find me using the term "trophy" buck. In my estimation, designating a deer as a trophy has nothing to do with the size of a buck's antlers. Every deer I have ever taken is a trophy to me. My best trophy to date is the first buck I shot, taken with my grandfather's single-barrel shotgun. It is every bit as much a trophy as the 24 point buck I shot a

15

few years ago -- and barely missed the Boone & Crockett Club's minimum listing by only a few points. It also is as much a trophy as the best scoring typical I have ever taken (a 26-inch wide eight point that also just missed the Boone & Crockett record book).

Were I required to define a trophy buck, my minimum would be a mature deer, four and a half years or older, with respectable antlers as large as, or larger than, the majority of bucks produced in the immediate area for that same age class. But, I also would classify a buck as a trophy if he were taken under extraordinary circumstances, or while hunting with a special friend.

Essentially, therefore, a trophy is in the eye of the beholder. You set your own standards. And that is as it should be.

Chapter 2

The Mature Buck

The campfire was down to the last embers. While the flames had burned high there had been loud and long discussions about the best whitetail caliber.

The oldest of our group maintained his devotion to the .270 Winchester. A couple of the younger guys championed the .300 Winchester Magnum, while still another insisted the 7mm Remington Magnum was without a doubt the finest whitetail rifle ever to have been built.

Of course, I knew all along the only real whitetail cartridge for a rifle was the .280 Remington -- well, at least until someone came up with something better, and I doubted they ever would! With that major problem solved, talk shifted to the bucks we had seen during the past two days of hunting.

In two days we six hunters had seen numerous bucks. Most bucks had been young -- the kind which would be hanging from the meat pole in many other camps. But only one deer had been taken thus far, an old craggy-antlered basic six point with a couple of non-typical points. He was a buck our group had been after for the past three years. The first time we saw him he had six points, and even then was a mature deer.

In the same area we also had seen several young bucks that looked as if they had come out of the same mold. On the ranch such bucks were not welcome and efforts were made to rid the ranch of such inferior antlered bucks. The young bucks had been relatively easy to take. The old one, now finally hanging from the meat pole, had taken quite a bit of doing.

Four of us had hunted the old master by every legal method, but he seemed to live a charmed life. He had been shot at and missed by two members of our group, missed by hunters who seldom fail to hit what they shoot at. The old patriarch just seemed to affect them the wrong way, even though he certainly was not a monster buck. But today, their shots had been accurate and the old six point's reign had come to an end.

A hunter's dreams

As the conversation wound on, the hunters started falling victim to the call of their sleeping bags. I successfully fought off the same urge, poured myself another cup of strong black cowboy coffee, and stretched out by the fire. Staring into the flames, I toasted the old six point. He had been a respected adversary. Not having him around to pursue left a bit of an emptiness in the camp.

The cold started to seep in as the glow of the coals diminished, yet the crisp cool of the night was refreshing to body and soul. I recalled other campfires, those enjoyed at Cross Creek Hollow in Alabama with J. Wayne Fears, and those shared with Ron Porter throughout Texas, as well as a host of other similar campfires in Georgia, Wyoming, Missouri, Tennessee, Canada and many places in between. All had been shared with special friends and acquaintances. All of us treasured a common dream and desire -- to take a mature whitetail with respectable antlers.

Hunting mature bucks also involves some maturity in the hunter. J. Wayne Fears enjoys not only a hunt for quality white-tailed deer, but also the time spent in the woods, either with other hunters or by himself.

18

Above, the Milky Way glimmered brightly in the dark December sky. What remained of the moon was about to disappear into the western horizon. Maybe tomorrow would be the day, the day to take a mature buck.

My mind drifted to the buck I had passed up earlier that morning. Had I been hunting elsewhere the four-year-old would have been shot at. On this particular hunt, however, he would not be in danger of being hunted until he was at least five or six years old.

Visions of great bucks with massive antlers, lots of points and wide spreads seemed to race across the sky. The cold finally awakened me, just in time for me to crawl into my sleeping bag for a few minutes before the alarm awakened me to another day of hunting.

First light was still only a promise when I headed to a distant part of the pasture. In years past I had seen several good mature bucks near a remote waterhole, my morning's destination. I intended to rattle horns shortly after the sun rose from its eastern bed of cactus and thornbush. With any luck I might be able to attract at least one buck worthy of taking.

I followed the faint trail to the edge of a nearly impenetrable thicket, wanting to set up for rattling nearby. (The day before I had made a cursory scouting trip through the area and found several scrapes and rubs.) Finding an area where I could see anything that might approach from the downwind side, I sat down and waited.

Drama at the scrape

As I was about to begin my rattling sequence a young eight point buck walked out of the dense thicket. Throwing any caution to the wind, he walked over to one of the scrapes I had found the day before and began nuzzling the overhanging limb. He then vigorously scraped the ground beneath the limb. This accomplished, he urinated on his tarsal glands and let it trickle to the ground below. The scrape freshened, he momentarily thrashed a nearby shrub with his antlers, then started moving down the trail.

Before he had disappeared completely another buck of nearly the same age and antler dimensions appeared out of the thicket and started a threatening advance toward the first. The bucks circled each other, their eyes bugged and ears pinched tightly against their necks, the hairs of their entire bodies standing on end to make them appear larger than life. I sat back and waited for the fight, thinking I would have the best seat in the house.

The two bucks, both appearing to be about two years of age, continued threatening each other. Suddenly from out of the brush strode a swollen-necked, black-hocked buck with a massive 10 point rack. He strode toward the two youngsters.

Immediately they forgot all about trying to be tough. A hard stare from the mature buck made them "cow down" and slink away from the larger buck. After a couple of moments both of the smaller bucks turned and ran. His mission accomplished, the big buck walked to the scrape, freshened it and then disappeared into the brush. Under other circumstances I would have taken him, but on this particular property I was content to see what would happen next.

I laid the rattling horns aside, satisfied to simply watch if any other bucks, or the one which had just left, might return to again work the scrape. The show was just beginning. During the next two hours I watched four other young bucks approach the scrape and freshen it. The bucks ranged in age from yearlings to three-year-olds. The young bucks approached cautiously, all the while keeping an eye out for any mature buck that might be in the area.

During the rest of the morning the only good mature buck I saw approached the downwind side of the scrape. He briefly stared at the scrape, tested the breeze blowing toward him and then disappeared, realizing the scrape had not been visited recently by a doe in search of courtship. Before the morning's hunt was over I

Two-year-old bucks seldom show the full signs of rut, those being extremely swelled necks and dark stained hocks.

saw numerous other bucks, including three I eventually rattled up. Yet I did not squeeze the trigger. The big bucks I was seeking never showed up.

The wariness of mature bucks

Research has found most scraping activity occurs after dark. Supposedly no less than 75 percent of all such scrape visitations take place under the cover of darkness. It also has been found that many of the older bucks only occasionally "work" their scrapes. They often approach the location from the downwind side, watch the scrape momentarily, then move on if they see no reason to check the scrape any further or to freshen it.

There is a strong belief among hunters and researchers alike, which is supported by research and many hours of observation, that mature bucks are different than younger ones. I am certain they are, for I also have seen instances which support that theory -- many, many times. Some authorities question whether or not deer remember past experiences and learn from them. I tend to believe they do.

Larry Weishuhn with a huge mature northern white-tailed buck. Such bucks are challenging to hunt.

For several years I oversaw and managed a ranch in the Texas Hill Country, the one mentioned in the introduction where lived a magnificent buck I called Yellow Four. The ranch was managed intensively to produce big bucks. The animals there had excellent genetic potential for antlers, had every possible nutritional advantage, and if they showed promise as yearlings they were allowed to mature and advance to old age. Part of the management program called for removing every yearling buck that displayed fewer than six points.

While I now question the wisdom of such a program, at the time we were working with a geneticist who was convinced only bucks with six or more points as yearlings (approximately 16- to 20-month-old bucks) eventually produced the best of antlers. In fairness to the geneticist we did produce some extremely large-antlered and bodied bucks. We also harvested mature (in this instance those older than four years of age) six, seven and eight point bucks. In addition we removed a large number of does each year as well. All this meant the remaining deer were exposed annually to a considerable amount of hunting pressure. Those deer, both bucks and does, which survived became masters of evasion.

Initially most of the selective hunting was done from baited (legal in that state) permanent blinds. In one of the pastures of the ranch there was a rocky outcropping. From it I could watch five different bait sites and blinds. Each of the blinds was equipped with dark curtains so the deer could not see inside under normal circumstances. The curtains had been added after the deer no longer came to a bait station, realizing a hunter crouched in the blind. Normally, whenever hunters were on the ranch, I disappeared to the rocky outcropping to observe the behavior of the deer around the blinds.

On the ranch, as mentioned, lived several extremely large bucks. But only a few ever were seen by hunters, and then only briefly. My routine was to put the hunters in the blinds at about three in the afternoon, and then go to "my" observation rock with binocular and spotting scope. I carried a handgun so I could feel like I, too, was hunting.

Young does and fawns generally were the first to appear when the timed automatic throw-feeders went off. After the first few days of the season, during which there was considerable shooting at young bucks with fewer than six points, the primary bucks that visited these bait sites were the two- and three-year-old bucks, with eight or more points. It was as if they recognized that the hunters would not be shooting at them. The mature bucks, however, were completely different from the rest of the deer in the herd. They were extremely wary and secretive.

Several times while sitting on my rock, I watched mature bucks in the brush near the blinds, out of site of the hunters sitting inside. The older bucks would approach from the downwind side, stand in the bushes and watch the blinds. I have watched such bucks stand statue-like for over 30 minutes as they kept constant vigil of the blind, testing the breezes for any sign of humans in the area.

If the buck felt a hunter was present, he disappeared into the brush and headed toward another feed station to do the same. If he found one where a hunter was not present, he cautiously walked to the feeder and ate. The mature bucks were never wrong in their evaluations. This is how they acted before the rut started. But even though one would expect them to change when they started chasing does, the rut brought very few changes.

There are those who think all bucks throw caution to the wind when the breeding season begins, that they go completely bonkers. Perhaps some bucks do, but not all of them!

At the same feed stations during the rut, the bigger mature bucks with the best antlers approach the feeders early in the morning or late in the afternoon. They position themselves along a trail, back in the brush where they will be unseen by hunters. As each doe walks by, a buck makes a gesture to check her interest in his sexual advances. If she seems disinterested, he simply waits for the next doe, until he finds one interested in his advances. When he does, the chase is on.

If at all possible he tries to keep her in sight, but if she runs toward the bait station the buck halts and waits until she leaves the area, or is chased into the brush by a younger buck. Then he again picks up her trail.

I have had opportunities to observe buck and doe behavior around these same areas after dark. After dark the mature bucks pay virtually no attention to the blinds, as if they know the blinds are unoccupied after dark. The only time I have seen mature bucks around a feed station (which included an automatic, timed throw feeder and a bulk, free-choice feeder filled with a balanced pelleted ration during the hunting season) was either during the middle of the day when there were no hunters in the pasture or after dark.

Not all mature bucks are huge, much depends upon the region where they live. This Coues whitetail is not large by regular whitetail standards, but is a good mature buck for his subspecies.

The ranch gave me many opportunities to observe mature bucks. In many ways the property was much more important as a research area than it was for hunting. It certainly made me appreciate the fact that mature bucks are completely different than other deer within the herd.

The disappearing bucks

Since 1978 I have worked with many different ranches to improve the quality of the habitat and the deer herds that reside there. These ranches have ranged in size from approximately 1,000 acres to nearly 100,000 acres. Some are surrounded by high fences, others are surrounded only by five-strand barbed wire fences. (I tend not to call the high fences deer-proof, because I have seen deer go over, under and through the 8-foot tall wire mesh fences.)

On the ranches I work with or manage for a quality deer herd, we conduct annual game surveys. The property's vegetation determines what census technique we use. Throughout much of southern Texas the brush is relatively thick but low. On such properties we use a helicopter as a highly mobile platform from which to conduct our survey.

While we certainly do not see all the deer present, we do observe a fair number of them. Whatever our margin error is, it seems to be constant from year to year. When we include the deer herd recruitment and subtract the number of deer harvested each year, the figures are close to what they should be the following year. At some of these same properties we have been conducting annual helicopter game surveys for seven years.

Each year as we conduct the surveys we see some extremely large, mature bucks on the various properties. But, few of these bucks are seen by hunters during the hunting season, and even fewer are ever taken. Yet, during the following year we again see the same big bucks. What happens to them and where they go during the hunting season remains a mystery. Do they become nocturnal, do they move only in the thickest of brush, or do they simply not move at all when hunters are in the field? To be honest, I am not sure.

One of the bucks I saw for several years in a row was easily recognizable because of a triangular white spot on his left shoulder. Each October, as we surveyed, we saw him in the southwest part of the ranch. Yet, during November and December, he normally was seen in the extreme northeast part of the ranch. The distance between the two sightings was 12 air miles.

Another of the bucks that was easily recognizable each year had very palmate main beams. Each hunting season he took up residence near a windmill, in a small pasture designed to trap cattle. The trap lay only a short distance from the rancher's headquarters -- and therefore was off limits to hunting.

Each fall the buck showed up about the first of November. He practically lived in the traps, which had plenty of natural browse, water and a fair number of does hanging around for a four month period. In the relatively small area, he had all he desired. In late

January, he again disappeared and would not appear again until the following fall. The buck never was taken by hunters and finally was killed by coyotes.

A mature buck on which we kept tabs for several years was one of the only living white-tailed bucks I have seen that appeared to possess a main beam spread wider than 30 inches. We watched him grow up from the time when we estimated him as a two-year-old with a 20-inch wide rack. The buck, upon turning six or seven years old, had a 30-inch plus spread with 10 long tines and two non-typical points near the base. He, too, was easily distinguishable.

The hunters on the ranch never saw that deer. Yet, every day during the hunting season as they went to hunt other parts of the property they drove right past where he usually lived. Each year when the season started, the buck moved from where he spent most of the year, to live in the horse pens next to the ranch caretaker's home -- about 100 yards from the hunters' camp. That buck, too, was never taken. Neither were his skull and antlers ever found. What a shame!

Still another of "our" bucks, a definite contender for the Boone & Crockett record book, lived in a small woodlot right next to a major highway. The buck spent his entire life in that little woodlot, only about a hundred acres in size. The only time anyone saw him was at night during the late summer, in the woodlot, when the farmer went there to check on his cattle. Several hunters hunted the deer, yet only one of them ever saw him -- during the middle of a day as the buck headed toward water.

Never take a big buck for granted

Pursuing mature or even over-the-hill bucks (more about that later) is a passion of mine and several of those I hunt with. And if there is one thing we have learned it is not to take mature deer for granted. Big bucks are different!

Several years ago J. Wayne Fears (fellow outdoor writer and wildlife biologist, as well as one of my favorite hunting partners) and I hunted on a large plantation in southern Alabama. The owners allowed a limited amount of hunting on the property and encouraged their hunters to take only mature bucks. My time to hunt the property was limited, but I deeply hoped for a chance at one of the bucks for which the area was known.

Based on the huge shed antlers and mounts on the wall, I finally had found the right place to hunt in Alabama. According to my host a massive, multi-tined buck had been seen several times browsing on roses in the backyard of an abandoned house, right on the edge of their property which ended at the city limits sign.

Many mature white-tailed bucks never develop huge antlers, but that does not make them any less challenging to hunt. Ron Porter shows off a hard won mature buck.

Over the evening meal one of the owners asked if I would mind hunting on the edge of town, practically in someone's backyard. I assured him I would hunt in the middle of town, sitting on top of the county courthouse, if it were legal and there were an opportunity at a buck like the one whose shed antlers he had shown me.

Long before daylight, my host dropped me off on the edge of the thigh-high grassy field between the city limits and a stand of planted pines. The previous afternoon, he had hung a climber tree stand on one of the trees. In only moments I found the tree and crawled up about 20 feet above the ground. From there I would have an excellent view of the grassy field, and the overgrown backyard and its rose bushes.

In the darkness I watched cars filled with hunters go driving by. I listened as town dogs yapped, cats yowled, and even a couple of roosters crowed. A light skim of fog hung in the air and the morning was cool. I hunkered deeper into my wool coat. To me it was one of those ideal Southern deer hunting mornings.

At first light I noticed movement beside the abandoned house. Through my binocular I could see a rather fair buck, a good eight point about three years old. He stood nibbling on one of the rose bushes. He was bigger than any whitetail I had ever seen in Alabama and I was sorely tempted to take a shot -- if only he would cross the fence. Just then I saw movement almost right under me.

Three does walked into the grassy field. Behind them walked a buck only slightly smaller than the one munching roses in the adjoining backyard. I brought up my rifle, peered through the scope and mouthed "bang." He appeared to be a 3-1/2-year-old. Had I been hunting anywhere else in Alabama, I would have shot him. But, I was hunting a particular deer, and I had promised the landowner not to shoot a lesser one. I was beginning to doubt the wisdom in making such a promise. The second buck momentarily checked the does, then headed toward the yard where I had seen the first buck.

When I left my stand at one o'clock that afternoon both bucks were bedded in that yard. Unfortunately, the big one did not show, and that afternoon I needed to travel to another lodge for some business.

I later learned my host took the buck a couple of days after I left. It had 16 points, arising from beams which had basal measurements over 6 inches in circumference. He shot the buck during the middle of the day, as it headed out of the planted pines and across the grassy field, probably to munch on roses.

According to my host on that hunt, he had tried to convince several clients and guests to hunt the buck, but none believed a buck of such monstrous proportions lived so close to town where it would have to contend with traffic noise and town dogs. Sometimes too much knowledge can be detrimental to hunters. Mature bucks are where you find them. Never take them for granted!

Bucks know how to fool a hunter

Only occasionally do mature bucks let themselves get caught in a sticky situation. Seeing how they react tells much about their finely honed instincts for survival.

A few years ago I had the opportunity to hunt on the famed Sanctuary in northern Michigan. Because bucks on this property are allowed to mature in the presence of ideal nutrition, this intensively managed land has produced some unbelievably huge bucks, both in body and antler size.

During the hunt, Skipper Bettis and I hunted an open area amid the tall trees not far from the luxurious camp. Just before first light we crawled into a large box blind built several feet off the ground. As the sun started to appear several Eastern wild turkey gobblers began gobbling, even though it was fall.

The morning began cool and crystal clear. In the first hour of daylight we saw only a couple of does and fawns. The only critters moving seemed to be the gobblers we had listened to earlier. I watched them occasionally through my binocular as they pecked at tidbits here and there, all the while heading generally in our direction.

During that first hour I figuratively had picked apart each bush, tree and log as I searched for deer. So while Skipper kept scanning the edges of the opening in the trees, I watched the progress of the turkeys. Just then, one of the gobblers jumped on what appeared to be a log.

When the gobbler leaped, a huge buck erupted out of the ground between two other logs. The gobbler spooked and so did the deer, but the buck quickly regained his composure. He slipped away with his head low to the ground, moving to an old snag between him and us.

Once behind the snag, he kept it directly between us. The only thing I could see of the deer were the outer sides of his massive, typical 12 point rack, protruding from either side of the snag. He moved directly away from us in that fashion until he disappeared into the dense underbrush. Not only was it amazing how the old buck used the snag to escape from us, it was also amazing that he would lie there, almost in plain view, not 40 yards from our blind.

Had the gobbler not literally stepped on the old buck, I doubt the deer would have ever moved. Had I not been watching at the exact time this happened, we never would have known the buck was anywhere close.

While on a muzzleloader hunt in the Midwest, I watched a truly nice eight point mature buck evade an experienced hunter. I

Young bucks such as this nice 8 point, if passed, will grow into monstrous bucks.

was sitting in a climbing tree stand where I could observe a green field. Not far away in a tripod was another hunter. The only thing separating us was the field and a brushy fenceline.

About an hour before dark I watched the buck approach the edge of the field and immediately spot the hunter. With one eye on the hunter the buck moved across the field. The entire time the hunter never looked my way. If he had the buck would have easily been in shooting range for him -- under 75 yards. From my position the buck was between 250 and 300 yards distant, out of range for the muzzleloader I carried. Besides, for much of the time the other hunter was directly in my line of sight and I would not have dared shoot, even if using my normal .280 Remington. When we met after legal shooting time, the hunter would not believe my story -- until I showed him the tracks.

Mature whitetails do not always come out on top. But they do quite often. In the case of the Midwestern hunter, he never would have known he'd been bested by the buck had I not been there to watch. All these instances make me wonder how many times something similar has happened when there was no one else to see a mature buck make a fool out of me.

Masters of evasion

During my years as a wildlife biologist I have had the opportunity to spend time on large properties which essentially allowed no hunting. It would seem reasonable that bucks, with no reason to fear humans, would not exhibit the same kind of wariness shown by a hunted buck. But, in fact, most are extremely wary and secretive. True, some show no fear at all and become very trusting. But such bucks are greatly in the minority.

One of the ranches at which I spent some time had not allowed any hunting for over 20 years. During that stay I saw quite a few really nice mature bucks, but not the number of huge bucks I had expected to see. Actually, I have seen more big mature bucks on well-managed hunting ranches than on those without hunting.

Much of this has to do with the quality of forage available to the deer. Where they are unhunted, populations increase to the point where the deer eat themselves out of house and home. The first to die of starvation are the old mature bucks and does, and the youngsters. The middle aged portion of the herd generally survives.

When this sort of die-off occurs, the habitat is adversely affected. Recovery takes a long time. Deer populations, however, recover much more rapidly. Such had been the case at the unhunted ranch.

While there had been a fairly high number of bucks in the herd, most had matured when forage conditions had been poor. During the habitat's recovery period, prairie grasses had responded more quickly than other vegetation, slowly turning the ranch to grassland. While white-tailed deer are ruminants (having stomachs with four compartments) just like cattle, they cannot convert most grasses to energy. Solid stands of grass crowded out broad-leaf forbs and other deer browse.

But there was one advantage to the tall grass. It provided great hiding places for mature deer. On that particular ranch I watched several bucks simply sink into the grass as we approached. When I walked to where one disappeared, all I found was more grass and no buck. Even though they were not being hunted, the mature bucks still were masters of evasion.

While hunting whitetails in the tall grass country of north Texas, and also in eastern Wyoming and Colorado, I have seen mature white-tailed bucks use the same tactics. It was often a case of now-you-see-them-now-you-don't.

Hunting on the spacious Nail Ranch in northwestern Texas, I have seen some extremely good bucks start running through a sea of knee-high bluestem grass. Sudden the buck drops to the ground as if shot and disappears into the tall grass. Several times I have hurried quickly to the spot where the deer disappeared, but could not find him. I have seen the same thing happen in eastern Colorado.

One of the best live typical bucks I have ever seen, I saw on a mule deer hunt southeast of Colorado Springs, Colorado. Soon after leaving camp the first morning we spotted five big white-tailed bucks chasing a doe. All of the bucks were extremely large-antlered, but one in particular easily would have exceeded the Boone & Crockett minimum for the typical category. He had 12 long tines, ranging in length from about 6 to 14 inches, with an estimated 24-inch spread.

The buck stopped, stared in our direction, then quickly disappeared into the tall grass and dried native sunflowers. One second he was there, the next he was gone. This in an area where there were relatively few whitetails. Unfortunately, we had seen the monstrous buck on property we had no permission to hunt.

On the last day of our hunt we gained permission to hunt the property next to where we had seen the huge typical. Sadly, by then I already had filled my tag with a very respectable mule deer, which was indeed the goal of our hunt. The morning's hunt yielded only sightings of mule deer and pronghorn antelope. However, extremely late that afternoon, with mere moments of legal shooting light left, we spotted a white-tailed doe running directly toward us across the tall grass prairie.

We sat hidden on a small rise which gave us a command of the entire grassy area below. The doe continued running toward us. Moments later we saw what she was running from, a really good white-tailed buck with at least 10 points and a 23-inch outside spread. The doe ran into a stand of sunflowers just below us, stopped and looked back at her trail -- probably to be sure the buck was still following. Indeed he was.

He came at a fast run. Just as he reached the sunflowers he glanced up at the ridge from where we watched. Immediately he dove into the thicket, lay down and stretched his head forward, resting it on the ground. Unfortunately for him, our angle offered an excellent shot for my companion. Moments later we were standing where the buck lay. He was even better than we had thought-not the big buck we had seen earlier, but a truly magnificent specimen for a mature white-tailed buck.

I certainly hope to have other opportunities at mature bucks such as that one, and hopefully they will occur before I already have filled my tag! But then, next time I certainly will know better.

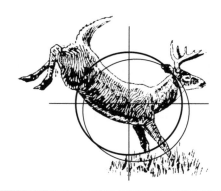

Chapter 3

Asking the Right Questions

During the latter half of the 1900s, North America has been transformed from a rural to an urban civilization. Most of today's deer hunters no longer live on the property they hunt. Deer hunters and nonhunters live primarily in cities and towns, far from hunting grounds.

Unfortunately this shift in population has bred an urban attitude, and with it much false information about wildlife and hunting. The greatest threat to all wildlife -- and thus a threat to hunting -- comes from the majority of the urban dwellers. The times they are a'changing!

In years past, hunters had considerable knowledge of the areas they hunted. When deer season was closed they hunted quail, grouse, squirrels and rabbits in the same areas they hunted deer. By spending plenty of time in the field, they had a fairly good idea as to the deer population and herd composition -- based on what they saw throughout the hunting season and the rest of the year.

The whitetail hunting explosion

Thankfully, in spite of today's urban shift, deer hunting still is extremely popular. In the early 1990s, estimates claimed more than 11,000,000 deer hunters in the United States. Seven times more sportsmen and women hunt deer than the next largest hunting activity. Interest in quality deer and quality hunting has never been greater.

Informal observations and research show an increasing number of hunters are interested in taking a quality animal. Because of outdoor and sport shows that display the better animals taken in an area each year, because of the volumes that are written about big whitetails, and because of the maturing deer hunting population, interest in big deer never has been higher or more intense than it is today. Increasingly more deer hunters are willing to pass up young bucks to hope and wait for an opportunity at a mature deer.

Several years ago most whitetail hunters hunted only in their home states, and only relatively close to home. This is rapidly changing. With their growing interest in taking big, mature white-tailed bucks, today's hunters are willing to travel far beyond their usual hunting areas or home states. Many are willing to spend large amounts of money to attain their goals. Costs of guided hunts for big white-tailed bucks rival those for huge bull elk.

For many years the glamour species to hunters have been animals such as bighorn sheep, elk and grizzly bears. While there still is considerable interest in those species, the tide has shifted and large antlered white-tailed deer have become *the* big game animal. Those who keep tabs of such things in the magazine publishing business tell me if they use a photo of a large whitetail on their cover, magazine sales jump dramatically, regardless of the time of year the publication appears on the newsstand.

Today we see magazines devoted strictly to the deer hunter and whitetail enthusiasts. Magazines such as *Deer & Deer Hunting* and others are extremely popular. Organizations and associations have been formed to focus solely on white-tailed deer. These include unified groups such as the Texas Trophy Hunters Association, Buckmasters, Whitetails Unlimited and the Quality Deer Management Association, among others.

How long all this interest will last is anyone's guess. However, white-tailed deer are the most widespread of our North American big game animals, and can be hunted in a great variety of terrain and habitat. They present an outdoor challenge regardless of where or how they are hunted.

This interest in whitetails has spawned a tremendous industry. Open any outdoor magazine and you will notice advertisements for deer hunting products of every sort. You also will notice the great number of hunting lodges, outfitters and guides that advertise their whitetail hunts.

In search of a better hunt

Bucks always seem bigger in the next county or state, or even nation. And sometimes they are! Each year hundreds of thousands of hunters travel to the far reaches of North America in search of big mature whitetails. Many travel great distances and have a successful hunt, taking the deer of their dreams. Others travel to new areas in search of a unique deer hunting adventure and find it. Still others, however, travel to areas and not only are disappointed and unsuccessful in taking a buck such as they had dreamed of, but have a miserable hunt that did not even approach their expectations.

Not all hunts or hunters are going to be successful in taking a huge mature deer, regardless of where they hunt. But that does not mean the hunt was not or should not be successful in terms of having an enjoyable time.

The best way to insure an enjoyable and successful hunt in a new area, or while hunting with a lodge, guide or outfitter, is to do your homework before committing to a hunt. Learn everything you can about the operation with which you are considering hunting. Learn as much as you can about their history of producing the kind of deer you are hunting -- and hopefully take. Talk to people who have hunted the area you are considering to hunt.

If something sounds too good to be true, double-check with others who have been there, because it may actually be too good to be true. If you receive information and want to verify it, contact the state's wildlife department and find out who the local game warden or wildlife biologist is for the area you are considering. Most states maintain at least a cursory record of the quality of deer taken in any particular area, based on age, weight and antler measurements.

Much can be learned by doing your homework before going on any hunt. Getting the facts is imperative as J. Wayne Fears is doing.

I cannot emphasize it enough. Always do your homework before hunting an area with which you are not already familiar through experience, regardless of whether it is a supposedly "proven" area, or one in which you are prospecting for bucks. More on the latter a little later.

A guaranteed disappointment

While returning from a trip to Alabama, I encountered a group of hunters in the Birmingham airport. Their accent revealed they were from the Northeast. I listened as they spoke of all the monster bucks they would see at the hunting camp they had reserved for the next five days. They continued talking about how they were looking forward to hunting during the rut. This would be their first time to do so. Each hunter voiced his intention to take the full limit of big bucks to which he was entitled. In Alabama that meant a legal bag limit of a buck a day.

I knew the history of the lodge where the group would be hunting. It was not large and had been hunted extremely heavily the past several years. The lodge's hunter success rate was extremely low and the average buck taken was a yearling. Because of the extremely heavy hunting pressure on this lodge and on the property surrounding it, few -- if any -- bucks were being allowed to advance beyond the yearling age class. To say mature bucks in the area were scarce would have been an understatement!

And what about their intentions to hunt during the rut? I did not have the heart to tell them they were about a month too late to hunt during the rut -- at least in the part of Alabama they would be hunting. Neither did I care to tell them that, in my occasionally hunting in Alabama, for the past several years I had yet to see a buck much bigger than a spike, with the one notable exception described in the previous chapter.

I visited with the hunters briefly, wished them well, then boarded a plane to Texas, there to hunt a ranch I knew had an abundance of bucks older than four and a half years. In fact, over 40 percent of the total buck herd were mature bucks. I also knew I would be hunting the ranch when the rut was about to start. How? I had done my homework before committing to the hunt. True, the ranch was only about 40 miles from my home and I knew the area well. Nonetheless, I had gotten in touch with the ranch owner/manager and asked some hard questions.

The above example is not meant to disparage Alabama, for it is a state I dearly love to visit during the hunting season. I enjoy their deer woods and the challenge of hunting there. Quite frankly, I have encountered similar groups and individuals in many other states (including in Texas) who unwittingly were approaching impending disappointment.

Several times future Texas deer hunters have called me to tell about the fantastic whitetail hunt they had booked in South Texas, and all the huge bucks they were going to see, and how they hoped to take the best one. In describing where they were booked to hunt, they mentioned areas far from what I would consider South Texas. Those areas actually are in Central Texas, or the Texas Hill Country, an area known for an abundance of deer. However, unless a person hunts on an intensively managed ranch, the chances of taking a deer like those taken on similar ranches many miles south is

extremely small. True, the ranches they had booked were south --
as opposed to Amarillo, situated in the far north part of Texas in
the Panhandle. Always do your homework!

In spite of usually practicing what I preach, I also have learned
the importance of homework the hard way. A few years ago two deer
hunting partners and I journeyed north of the U.S.-Canada border
for the chance to take a huge Canadian white-tailed buck. We had
heard much about the particular area from mutual friends who
had hunted there. They told glowing tales of big bucks in every
woodlot and field.

With little further regard, we booked a hunt with the outfitter they
had suggested. Each passing day we dreamed of the big bucks we
would take while in Canada. Surely the three of us would each take
a record book contender!

When we finally reached camp, our outfitter/guide said he would
place us in areas where we would have an excellent chance of seeing the buck of a lifetime. He then instructed us we were not to get
out of deer stands for any reason. His assistant would drop us off
at the base of the tree stand and later return to pick us up. For two
days we hunted hard, practically from daylight to dark. But, we did
not spot a single deer. Nothing.

Each night snow fell, but after the third day we compared notes
and discovered no one in camp had seen a fresh track. The morning
of the fourth day (of the five day hunt) we left our tree stands and
started searching for fresh deer sign. None was found by any in our
group.

Over lunch that day we confronted the outfitter with what we suspected: there were no deer in the area. After considerable hemming
and hawing, he finally admitted our chances of seeing a deer, any
deer, were extremely remote. The previous winter the deer herd had
experienced an extensive winter kill and few deer remained in the
area.

Should the outfitter have called us before our arrival and can-
celled the hunt? Most definitely! However, long before we left Texas,
a quick call to the provincial game department also would have
been in order. Had we done our homework, the expense of the totally miserable hunt could have been avoided and prevented. But
because we wanted something so badly, we failed to do our homework and check on the simple things.

Homework is not just for kids

Nowadays I do my deer hunting homework regardless of where I
travel to hunt, be it only a few miles from home or across the continent. Not only does homework insure a successful hunt, but the
information learned is invaluable.

Because of my interest in primarily hunting mature bucks, I desire to hunt where such age class bucks exist in considerable numbers. Thus, before making plans to hunt any new area, I make a list of questions I want answered by the person who runs that hunt. If I doubt the answers, especially if they sound too good to be true, then I will query several other people who have hunted the same area. I also will ask for a list of both successful and unsuccessful hunters who have hunted there.

Here is the list of questions I usually ask:

1. Is your operation under a quality deer management program, or within a quality management unit? If yes, how long have you been involved in such a program?

2. What is the name of the biologist who oversees your management program and how can I get in touch with him or her?

3. How large an area do you hunt?

4. What steps do you take to improve the deer's nutrition? Do you fertilize food plots annually?

5. What is your total deer density (expressed in acres per deer) and what methods do you use to determine your density?

6. What is your current buck-to-doe ratio?

7. What has been the fawn survival rate the last five years?

8. What percentage of the bucks are older than three and a half years of age?

9. What is your overall hunter success rate?

10. What percentage of your hunters take bucks older than three and a half years of age?

11. Can you provide a list of the deer taken by your hunters which includes information about the deer's age, weight, number of points, length of tines, basal circumferences, length of main beams, and outside spreads?

12. How many bucks do you harvest each year?

13. How many does do you harvest each year?

14. What kinds of bucks can I expect to see during the hunt?

15. What kind of buck can I reasonably expect to take during the hunt?

16. When is the best time to hunt for a good deer at your operation?

17. How will we hunt?

18. Is the area you hunt prone to winter-kill or to extended droughts? If so, when did the last ones occur?

19. What is the name and address of the local state wildlife biologist or game warden?

Answers to the above questions are important to a good decision. Most quality whitetail hunting operations can supply these answers, and their proprietors are happy and proud to do so. Biologists and managers involved in quality deer management programs usually are eager to talk about what they are doing, and have considerable records to support the information they provide. If someone you contact about a hunt is reluctant to provide this sort of information, it may be best to look elsewhere. However, the possible exception is when you are prospecting new and unproven areas for big bucks.

Interpreting the information

Receiving such information is great, but interpreting it correctly is equally important. Many of today's deer hunting areas, whether private or public, have a management program. The program's goal may be to produce the most possible deer for maximum hunter recreation. Another program may strive to produce an abundance of bucks over three and a half years old. If the latter is the case, find out how long such a program has been in place.

If such a program has been in use only a year or two, chances are slim that an abundance of mature deer exists. Such a program should be in place at least three years before its results become apparent.

Most deer herds have the genetic potential to produce bucks with big antlers -- if they are allowed to mature in the presence of proper year-round nutrition. In certain areas of the continent deer have high quality forage available during the spring and early summer. In areas with many mast-producing trees, deer enjoy a high energy feed source that helps them put on fat for the winter. The most critical times for most deer herds are late summer, when the quality of forage is fairly low, and late winter when available forage is extremely low in nutritional quality.

For antler development the most critical period is winter. Bucks are trying to recover from the rigors of breeding season, a time when some bucks may lose as much as 25 percent of total body weight. If they lack sufficient forage during this time, they face a high chance of death from malnutrition.

Plantings of supplemental forage, such as green fields and food plots, can provide the nutrition bucks require during this time. That is why knowing these are available to deer on the property you plan to hunt can be important.

Deer densities normally are expressed in terms of acres per deer or deer per section (640 acres). Understand there is no one ideal deer density when choosing a hunting area for mature bucks. The density should depend upon the year-round food availability. An extremely high density of one deer per five acres simply may mean the area has many deer, but if the forage quality and quantity are inadequate, that heavy population may not yield any sizeable deer.

Buck-to-doe ratios indicate the composition of the deer herd. If I am seeking to take a mature deer, I usually want to hunt where the buck-to-doe ratio is no wider than one buck per three to four does. However, I prefer to hunt where the ratio approaches one buck to two does, or even fewer does.

Many of the deer herds we manage for quality have a one-to-one ratio. This means that if the deer herd is in tune with its habitat and food supply there will be quite a few bucks.

As to the percentage of bucks within the herd that are at least three and a half years of age, this figure should approach 40 percent or more of the total buck population in the area.

The fawn survival rate indicates the potential of the deer herd's recruitment. If few fawns are born one year, then three years later there will be few three-year-olds.

The small number of fawns born one year can be traced through the deer herd and the harvest for many years thereafter. Several years ago our region of Texas experienced a horrible extended drought and virtually no fawns survived for two years. Four and five years later few really good bucks existed in our part of the country. They were neither seen nor harvested by hunters, because the mature age classes simply did not exist. Unfortunately, few hunters ask about the fawn survival rate, yet it can be of paramount importance for someone interested in hunting mature bucks.

On most properties I have been involved with that manage for quality deer, we conduct an annual game survey -- actually several surveys. We gather data relative to total deer density (bucks, does and fawns); adult density (bucks and does, expressed in acres per deer); buck-to-doe ratios; fawn survival rate; number of bucks that are young, middle aged and mature; total number of bucks observed within each basic antler point category, from spikes to 12 points; and any other information we can about the deer herd and the habitat.

From this data we determine the number of bucks and does to be harvested annually. On such properties, essentially every buck taken will be at least three and a half years old. The possible exception is the allowing of a young hunter to take a smaller buck.

In selecting a place to hunt mature whitetails, I look for a property where the vast majority of the bucks taken are at least three and a half years of age. I also request the number of bucks taken from the property each year, and also the number of does. If the operation is not taking does, then I will question why this is the case. Only in rare cases should the annual doe harvest not equal the buck harvest. If that is not happening, then question their claims.

If the answers to my questions reveal a high incidence of yearling bucks taken in the harvest, I know that most of the bucks are being harvested before they are more than a year and a half old. I therefore will look elsewhere.

Most operations that provide quality hunts for mature deer, maintain extensive records, including aging and measuring every deer taken. Most are proud to provide such information to potential hunters, if asked. This information will give you better insight of what has been taken, but also will give you some idea as to the type of buck you should hunt for and have reasonable expectations of taking.

If the outfitter tells me the best time to hunt is right before or during the rut, then that is when I will try to make arrangements to be there. There are several advantages to hunting during the rut. There also are several advantages to hunting early in the season, at the first legal opportunity. If I am uncertain of the dates of the rut in an area I am considering hunting, a call to the state or province's wildlife department will confirm this and other information.

If I have confidence in a lodge manager or outfitter/guide, and he has proven his expertise during phone calls, I will pay attention to how he tells me to hunt. He is the local expert and knows what methods and techniques have proven successful. By paying attention to what he and his crew suggest, my chances of success will be greatly enhanced.

Prospecting for whitetails

Earlier I mentioned prospecting for big whitetails. This not only can be great fun, but rewarding as well. Whitetail populations are increasing throughout North America, and they are expanding into new areas. This is especially true along the eastern edge of the Rockies, as well as in other areas.

In an earlier chapter I mentioned seeing a monstrous white-tailed buck in eastern Colorado. The local landowner was hardly aware of the whitetail's presence. When I asked him if there were any whitetail on the ranch, he stated he had seen one only on rare occasions. He also doubted there were more than five or six on the entire ranch. During five days of hunting, however, I saw 21 different white-tailed bucks and nearly twice that many does and fawns!

Whitetails are appearing in areas where they previously were nonexistent, or at best extremely rare. These new areas often produce monstrous bucks. Finding them, however, is not easy. Good resources include county agricultural extension agents, rural mail carriers, rural school bus drivers, game wardens and wildlife biologists. These people are in the field during early morning hours when deer tend to move. They also have opportunity to talk with many people who live in the country and who work and travel through those areas.

A friend of mine spends his free time "cowboying" on several ranches in areas where there are supposed to be no whitetails. Yet, in the past five years he has taken five massive, multi-tined white-tailed bucks. According to him the whitetails live in brushy creek bottoms in this otherwise wide open prairie country. I am certain at least one of his bucks easily would meet the Boone & Crockett whitetail minimum, yet he prefers to not have them officially scored and registered (so he can maintain anonymity).

Weishuhn visits with a rural mail carrier about the bucks he has been seeing during his early morning delivery routes. Information from such individuals is invaluable.

The reason for my friend's success? He prospected for this "mother lode" of whitetails. However, he is quick to point out there are still many more unexplored pockets of deer left, and to make matters ever more interesting, these undiscovered areas are increasing in number every day!

With doing your homework for finding places to hunt mature deer come several responsibilities. Primarily, these responsibilities include learning how to shoot accurately and becoming intimately knowledgeable of your firearm or archery equipment. When you finally get within shooting range of a majestic whitetail you owe it to him to make a quick and humane kill.

One of the most frequent complaints I hear from people who outfit and guide whitetail hunters is that the majority of these hunters do not know their firearms or how to shoot them accurately. Avoid being the subject of such gossip.

Long before hunting season starts, spend considerable time at the range getting acquainted with your firearm or bow. Know exactly where it will strike the target at varying distances. Learn to know the limitations of your firearm or your bow, but also know your own. Should a shot be "iffy," don't take it!

Throughout this book, I will refer primarily to hunting deer with firearms -- rifles, shotguns, handguns and muzzleloading rifles. I also am a strong supporter of bow hunting and bow hunters -- I have hunted and taken mature whitetails with a bow, and likely will again pursue them with archery equipment. However, my preference is to hunt deer with a firearm. The smell of burnt gunpowder mixed with aroma of the fall deer habitat is the sweetest and most attracting perfume I have ever encountered.

Chapter 4

Travels of the Mature Buck

The buck was on the move, walking steadily at a determined pace with a distant destination in mind. Though unsure where he was headed, I planned to follow him as long as possible to see if I could find out.

The big eight-point was a mature buck, big of body and heavy of horn. His hocks were stained dark brown, from his tarsals nearly to his ankles. I first saw him at a distance as he moved at an easy pace, more or less in a straight line. He passed right by my hiding place at about 10 a.m. and kept moving into the slight northerly breeze. How long he had been walking or how far he had already come, I did not know. After he passed, I began to follow him.

In the open savanna grassland of the southern part of Texas, keeping up with him was easy. The ranch was quite large and I did not mind spending the day learning from the animal -- whatever he could teach me about mature buck behavior and movement.

The buck did not veer from his course as he covered approximately a mile every 20 to 30 minutes. He halted only to stare at another buck that crossed his path or to work any scrape he encountered, then continued on his way. During the four hours that I followed him the buck walked no fewer than eight miles in a straight line. I had to leave him because he crossed the ranch's boundary fence. Where he went I will never know. Nor do I know from where he came. No one else ever reported having seen him.

I often have hunted on a 45,000 acre ranch in that same part of Texas, I frequently have seen bucks that were observed only once and then never again. Most of the time these were bucks acting in a manner similar to that of the big eight-point. They seemed to be heading some place in particular and were just passing through with no intention of taking up residence. Not all such bucks in this area act similarly to the big eight-point, but there always have been a few. I suspect bucks like him exist anywhere there are whitetails.

Other bucks on that same property often can be found quite close to the same area. Still other bucks seem to show up in the same area again and again, sometimes every three to five days in the same spot. Such was the case with a particularly large buck I watched for one deer season. Every third day, the buck showed up in the same area, always near a thicket in the center of the property. That was the only place or time that particular buck was seen.

Why deer travel

Deer in many ways are like people. Each and every one is an individual, a little different than the next, not only in the way it looks -- including antler development -- but also in the way it acts and reacts. The same holds true in the way a deer moves throughout its habitat.

Deer move primarily for one of two reasons: to search for food and water, or to have sex. These are the major motivators. But just as people, some are born, live their entire lives and die in a small locale.

Mature bucks are individuals; some tend to roam during the rut, while others are homebodies.

Some seem to continue moving throughout life. Others grow up in an area, move to a new location, then spend the rest of their lives there. Still others may spend a fair amount of time somewhere, leave for a while, then return. And the possibilities continue. Deer simply are as individual as you and I.

With the advent of reliable radio telemetry equipment (in which a radio transmitter is attached to a deer and then followed to determine its movement within any study area), much has been learned about the travels of mature white-tailed bucks. Formerly it was believed that every deer is born, lives and dies within the one square mile, approximately 640 acres, regardless of its region. In some instances and under some specific circumstances that may certainly be true. But not in all cases.

In a research project on a large ranch in South Texas, conducted by Dr. Steve Demarais, Bob Zaiglin, and a host of graduate students from Texas Tech University, radio collars were attached to several mature bucks -- including some with extremely large antlers. These bucks then were tracked to determine the distances they traveled from where they were captured, where they normally spent their time (their "home range"), and how and where they moved during the breeding season in relation to where they lived most of the rest of the year. The results, extremely interesting, proved what several of us in South Texas had been saying for several years. Mature bucks, at least in that part of the country, tended to roam over greater distances than one square mile.

According to this research mature bucks tended to have large elliptically shaped home ranges where they spent most of their time. Some of the bucks tended to spend the entire year in a relatively small area, less than 1,000 acres. At the other end of the spectrum, however, one buck roamed over an area in excess of 10,000 acres.

Some of the mature bucks tended to spend most of their spring, summer and early fall in one area, then shift to another area for the fall breeding season. They would remain in that area until they had cast their antlers, then move back to their "summer" ranges. Other bucks tended to be homebodies, staying in one area most of the time, but then for some unknown reason, simply leave the area for several days, and then return to their home area only a few days later. The average home range of the 14 radio-collared bucks in this study (with an average age of better than six years) exceeded 3,000 acres.

The terrain in which the research was conducted is quite consistent throughout, its vegetation being mostly low-growing brush, trees, cactus and shrubs. Primarily the research area is rangeland and only lightly stocked with cattle. The deer population, during the time the research was conducted, remained virtually unhunted.

While this project's results might not give a true picture of what happens elsewhere in different habitats and deer populations, it does give us some insight into what mature bucks do under those specific conditions and circumstances. It also proves mature deer are individuals and that they are not all the same!

In an upcoming chapter, summer scouting and early season hunting will be discussed. The movement of deer within their territories has a definite bearing on such scouting and hunting. The research conducted by Demarais and Zaiglin explains why, in some instances, bucks often are seen frequenting the same areas during the summer, but then seem to disappear as the breeding season approaches.

For example, suppose a farmer sees a buck in basically the same part of his land all summer long. He passes the information on to the hunters who hunt the property. By the time the gun season opens, the hunters spend many hours looking for the particular buck the farmer has told them about, yet they never see him. Could it mean that the buck has moved to another area because of natural movement? Possibly. But, it also could mean the mature buck has changed its habits because of too much pressure on the area. Therefore, he probably has not left the area, but has changed when and how he travels.

When and where mature bucks travel is determined by many different factors relating to food and sex. Many states have conducted a variety of deer movement research projects. Copies of those findings are available from the various state wildlife departments and from the major universities involved in such projects. Food availability, weather conditions, deer densities and buck-to-doe ratios, as well as hunting pressure, can cause deer to alter their travel distances, routes, and the times of the day they move.

To study the relationship of hunting pressure and deer movement, several years ago a group of deer were radio collared (for a telemetry study) at Missouri's northeastern Deer Ridge Wildlife Man-

When hunting mature bucks, hunters such as Kim Hicks, are constantly watching for deer and signs of big deer. It pays to be attentive at all times.

agement Area. The study area was approximately 3,900 acres in size. The rolling hills consisted of stands of oak and hickory trees, overgrown old fields, row crops, food plots, hayfields and pasture land.

During the two-year study, conducted by Brian Root, 24 whitetails (of which two were mature bucks) were radio collared and monitored for three nine-day periods, during the preseason, firearm season and postseason. During the season the area was hunted for nine days, during which the hunter density amounted to approximately 43 hunters per square mile. According to the study, does that normally traveled between 2 and 2.5 miles each day before the hunting season opened suddenly were moving 3 miles per day after the season opened. And regardless of the hunting pressure, they did not leave or alter their home range, or go into areas with which they were unfamiliar.

Bucks in the study reacted to similar hunting pressure by moving much more erratically than before the opening of the hunting season. However, the amount of their movement did not change due to hunting pressure. They ranged from 4 to 5 miles per day, regardless of whether or not hunters were in the woods. Neither did they alter their movements because of hunting pressure, although their home ranges generally were three times those of the does. One adult buck covered an area of over five square miles.

Although the bucks may not have moved from areas of heavy hunting pressure, this does not mean they did not somewhat alter their patterns. For instance, the researcher describes a hunter walking right past a collared and bedded buck. The buck was bedded in a brushy fence row and allowed the hunter to approach to within 25 feet of the hiding place. The hunter never saw the buck. The buck supposedly remained bedded for 10 minutes after the hunter passed by, but a half hour later was tracked over a half mile away.

It must be noted that the hunting season for this project, though intensive, was only nine days long and deer were not subjected to lengthy daily hunting pressure as they are in some areas.

Other deer researchers have suggested that movements and home range sizes of bucks increase under intensive hunting pressure, while still other researchers suggest just the opposite. All these opinions probably confirm that, as suggested earlier, deer may well be individuals and they behave in different manners in different areas and under other circumstances.

In the area of Missouri where the aforementioned research was conducted, hunters believed that whenever the hunting season started the local bucks headed to the safety of a refuge. But the local research did not indicate that bucks moved to another area when hunting pressure increased. Instead, they stayed in the same area and contended with hunters the best they could. That is a way of saying they learned how to evade hunters in the habitat which they intimately knew, knowing every possible hiding place and escape route.

The subjects of that research included two yearling bucks. One of those two bucks left the research area where he had been born and essentially grown up. He was shot by a hunter 76 miles northwest of where he had been radio-collared. While that is quite a distance, it is not unusual for yearling bucks to travel great distances when such bucks disperse in the fall.

Research conducted in Virginia's Shenandoah National Park by John Scanlon and Michael Vaughn showed bucks close to the area most used by people had a home range of 4,615 acres, while bucks in the back country had a home range of 3,965 acres. Bucks in both areas traveled a maximum distance of 3.8 miles per day. (Of the two mature bucks included in the study, one roamed widely during the breeding season, and the other had a restricted breeding territory. During the rut both moved from 1.2 to 1.8 miles per day.) Some deer hardly ever, or never, used any of the areas frequented by humans.

On the other hand, in a study conducted in the bottomlands of the Yellowstone River in Montana, Jim Herriges found deer were not noticeably affected by human activity. One of his radio-collared deer regularly was found bedded right next to an extremely busy road. Still another lived close to a house with dogs. In that study one of the mature bucks had a home range of 6.24 square miles, made up of upland draws and agricultural fields. Many of the deer in this study used the river bottom for bedding areas and traveled to alfalfa fields to feed during the night, often spending nearly five hours in the fields before returning before daylight to bed in the thickets along the river.

In a study conducted in southern Mississippi by Dr. Harry Jacobson and Carol Burns, deer in the study area did not shift their home ranges (of 909 to 4,205 acres) to take advantage of forage crops. This should be remembered when planting food plots, because it demonstrates the effectiveness of many small food plots rather than one large one.

In other areas, however, such as in Texas where one of our ranches had an irrigated food plot, we regularly observed marked deer traveling great distances (2 to 3 miles) to forage areas planted specifically for deer. Do you think deer just might be individuals, or that they may act and react differently in different areas? Methinks so!

How bucks use cover

Deer, especially mature bucks, learn quickly to take advantage of whatever cover is available to them. To say they are highly adaptable, would be an understatement.

In Illinois, where corn is king, a research project was conducted in an area characterized as one of the world's most intensively farmed areas. The only trees in the area are found in small woodlots, narrow shelter belts and along rivers and streams. In a research project headed by Charles M. Nixon, 38 bucks and 58 does were fitted with radio transmitters. These were tracked for four days each week.

The research indicated bucks tended to remain in cornfields for extended periods of times. One three-year-old buck hardly left a cornfield for a month at a time. Other bucks stayed in the cornfield for as long as three and four days without leaving, bedding during the day and feeding at night.

For a while Nixon and his group tracked 10 bucks that were three years or older. He noted the mature bucks moved into open cover during the time they were developing antlers to protect themselves from injury. According to him they also moved to open areas where they could maintain visual contact and interact with other local bucks -- to establish social dominance well before the beginning of the breeding season.

In his report, Nixon wrote that the ranges occupied by the older bucks were made up primarily of row crops, or sometimes flood-plain bottomland forests with little underbrush. In his opinion corn and soybeans were much less a threat to developing antlers than the dense underbrush present in many ranges occupied by bucks during the fall and winter. However, this is not necessarily the case in other areas, especially such as southern Texas where dense brush is the primary habitat and deer must learn to tolerate it, whether they are developing antlers or are in "hard" antler.

While the corn was standing, the deer in the area used it for cover, and scattered throughout the fields whenever danger threatened. After the corn had been harvested, deer tended to move to different areas. Because of this the home ranges of some bucks were highly variable, depending upon available cover. Ranges of mature bucks varied from 1,900 acres to 2,870 acres.

Interestingly, the Illinois study supported the theory that deer do not necessarily, in response to hunting pressure, move to a refuge where there is no hunting. Rather, the Illinois deer sought dense thickets where they could hide during the daylight hours, instead of moving great distances.

In chapter two I related numerous experiences with mature bucks I have observed on hunts, as well as on ranches I have managed throughout the country. Several of those bucks had learned to take advantage of cover close to human activity. Others had moved great distances, perhaps to avoid confrontation with hunters -- or perhaps they would have done it even if there had been no hunting on the properties. I cannot provide an answer as to why these deer acted as they did. While I can measure what deer do and where they move, I can only speculate as to why they do certain things.

Mature bucks are where you find them. Often good places to look for them are where other hunters do not expect them to be.

The big antler, low testosterone theory

For over 25 years I have had the opportunity to hunt many different areas and to talk with many hunters and deer researchers. I also have had the opportunity to examine a great many whitetail racks, including some of the largest and finest in the world. In addition, I have had the opportunity to admire some of the huge whitetail racks gathered by antler collectors. I have noticed that many of these really big, high-scoring racks have non-typical points, which, if the buck had done much fighting or rubbing, surely would have been broken. Yet even some of the thin extra-typical tines are seldom broken.

The lack of breakage among these types of points raises some interesting theories. Some students of deer behavior say the extremely large, multi-tined bucks have few broken tines because deer with huge antlers seldom have to fight. According to this school, a really big-antlered buck simply is accepted as the lord and master in a given area.

Personally I have trouble believing this. I have seen instances where the dominant and most aggressive buck in a given area is a big eight point with a large body. Such a buck does not mind fighting and will take on any deer, big-bodied, big-antlered or big-whatever. I thus strongly suspect the reasons why large-antlered bucks do little rubbing or fighting have little to do with their impressive racks.

Canadian professor Valerius Geist has noted that some huge-antlered and bodied mule deer produce only enough testosterone to get them through the antler development cycle, but not enough to make them sexually active during the rut. Such a deer would enter the breeding season in excellent shape. However, he would not be overly interested in chasing does, and thus would not lose any weight due to the rigors of the rut and fighting with other bucks. Thus, he would be in excellent body condition after the breeding season, and therefore enjoy a great start on the next year's antler development.

In addition, antler tines of a buck producing such a low level of testosterone would have a tendency to break during extensive rubbing, sparring or fighting. But being less concerned about reproduction, he likely would be more concerned about survival and thus devote greater time and energy to those endeavors, thereby exposing himself to less danger. This theory makes for some interesting speculation, does it not?

During the rut mature bucks seem to be constantly on the move.

Dr. Harry Jacobson, a Mississippi researcher, also has speculated about these occurrences in whitetails. After measuring testosterone levels of some of the largest white-tailed bucks taken in the Southeast, he found some of the truly huge-racked bucks tended to have a lower testosterone level than those with somewhat smaller racks -- of the same age taken in the same areas.

This finding makes sense to me. Excuse my sounding redundant here, but the matter bears repeating. Imagine a mature buck whose body produces just enough male hormones to see him through the normal antler growing season. He therefore does not chase does and is much more concerned about self-preservation than procreation. That being the case, he is in excellent body condition when the time of the breeding season ends. He casts his antlers and is in ideal body condition to start developing his new rack. I have seen white-tailed bucks that I am certain fit into that category.

What has all this to do with movement of mature bucks? Perhaps a great deal. The buck I just described likely would move very little during the hunting season, and regardless of whether he lived in the creek bottoms of the Plains states, in the deep woods of the North, in the hardwood bottoms and pine plantations of the Southeast, or in the arid brush country of the Southwest, he truly would be a super challenge to take.

Learning about the travels of mature bucks is challenging, frustrating, enjoyable and a whole lot of other adjectives. The best way to learn about the movement of deer is to spend considerable time doing your homework. This includes reading widely, asking questions, and getting into the field and scouting throughout the year, whenever possible.

Chapter 5

Postseason and Preseason Scouting

The seminar room had filled to the point of standing room only, filled with hunters and whitetail enthusiasts. In the back stood a uniformed game warden. They were attending a Southeastern stop for the National Rifle Association's Great American Hunters, and they listened attentively.

As the speaker on the podium, I was discussing the merits of scouting outside of the hunting season. In so doing I mentioned that I hunted deer all year long. I paused for a moment and gazed intently at the game warden. Predictably, he seemed surprised by my statement.

Before he could further react, I explained that I hunted deer throughout the year, but with a gun only during the hunting season. During the rest of the year I hunted deer to learn more about them and thus increase my chances of success during the fall when I was carrying a gun. The warden seemed to relax a bit, relieved that I did not shoot deer year round. After the session, he and I discussed my strategy of hunting throughout the year, for he too was interested in improving his opportunities at bigger bucks.

The postseason "hunt"

After the hunting season closes I usually wait a week or two, then head back to the areas I hunt. I am fortunate in that several of the properties I hunt are within a day's drive of my southwest Texas home -- but not all. More about that later.

Deer do not take long to return to their normal routines after the hunting season closes. On some of the properties I hunt in southern Texas the hunting pressure is extremely low, for we take only one mature buck per 500 acres. Thus the deer never really have a reason to change their normal routines, outside of the rut. Even on properties that are hunted quite heavily, most deer return to their normal routines in a week or two after the hunting season has closed. As soon as this happens I start my postseason scouting.

Several years ago I started to keep notes of sightings of deer and deer sign on the places I hunted. These records were maintained in a journal, now known as my "buck journal." In addition I mark sightings of deer and deer sign on a map of the property. Such maps, either topographical or aerial photo, are generally available from the landowner, or through the local Soil Conservation Service office or U.S. Geological Survey. Thanks to satellite technology, maps showing the various vegetation types and land uses will soon be available. Some of the early versions I have seen of these will show almost everything except the deer -- and some of the later maps will do just that, if you have the right viewing equipment.

The information gathered about your hunting "place" can be recorded on a map, especially where rubs, scrapes, and shed antlers are found.

As soon as possible after the hunting season, I start looking for deer and deer sign. During the winter I concentrate my search on winter food supplies, be they planted fields or areas that seem to attract deer because of native browse. I do this because bucks are particularly hungry after the rut. They must eat as much as possible to regain valuable weight lost during the breeding season. This actually is one of bucks' most critical stress periods.

Once hunting season has closed, bucks are more apt to show themselves in areas where they normally live and to leave cover earlier in the afternoon. This, therefore, is an extremely good time to locate deer and gain an idea of where to find them in the following hunting season. Postseason scouting trips also are a good time for locating rubs and scrapes, and to spend considerable time in the area where deer you hunt each fall actually live. Record all this information in your own "buck journal" or notebook.

The postseason offers a good opportunity to photograph bucks in the area you hunt. As I mentioned they tend to be extremely hungry during this time, and generally will tolerate humans within the area where they live without becoming completely nocturnal or leaving the area. If you can locate a good food source, such as green field, or perhaps what remains of a standing crop such as corn or another cereal grain, chances are excellent you will find deer very close.

The postseason is a time when few hunters are in the field. The weather is often cold, or at best miserable, and other activities beg for attention. My postseason scouting trips therefore are not as frequent or as long as I would like them to be. Nonetheless, I try to gain every advantage, and being in the field after the hunting season is one of the ways I can learn about deer, and especially mature bucks, without scaring them into altering their routines, or becoming fully nocturnal.

Scouting for shed antlers

Depending where you live, bucks start casting (shedding) their antlers in late January, early February, or even into late April. If my working schedule has allowed only a little postseason scouting dur-

A "buck journal" is an ideal place to record not only your hunts, but also your spring and summer scouting trips data.

ing the winter, I get serious about scouting just before spring greenup. By doing so I still can readily see shed antlers before the growing vegetation obscures them. If my working schedule prevents my entering the woods as soon as the bucks start dropping antlers, I wait to do it during the spring turkey season. That way I can enjoy hunting turkeys in the morning and then spend the rest of the day seeking shed antlers and other deer sign.

Shed antlers are hard evidence that a buck lived in a certain area for at least a period of time during the previous winter. The presence of relatively fresh sheds reveals that the buck which cast them survived the hunting season and that he should still be alive.

Sheds can provide much information, especially if you find the buck's shed for several years such as these being held by ranch manager Jimmy Perlitz (in hat) and Bill Whitfield, hunting consultant.

But more can be learned by the presence -- or absence -- of sheds, and by their condition. To begin, consider what the *absence* of shed antlers means. To some hunters it might indicate a complete absence of bucks within an area, and in some cases that might be an accurate conclusion, but it likely is not. In some areas few sheds are found because of tall vegetation. The lack also may indicate that most of the bucks found in the area are relatively young and never have had the chance to mature and develop big antlers. A combination of considerable ground vegetation and a young deer herd are two of the primary reasons for not being able to find sheds.

In several instances I have hunted sheds in areas where I was told they were impossible to find and that looking for sheds was a waste of time. (Of course, I do not consider any time spent in the field trying to learn about whitetails as a waste of time.) In such areas I have found either few sheds or virtually none. Checking the harvest records in those areas revealed that 80 percent of the bucks taken were yearlings. That, obviously, left few bucks to become two-year-olds, or even to cast their first set of antlers -- which could be found as shed antlers. This generally is the reason no sheds exist in an area.

I have hunted in areas where the above situation prevailed. True to form, I spotted primarily yearling bucks -- most of which were shot by the next hunter who saw them. I also have hunted in similar areas after members of a nearby hunting club instituted a quality deer management program, thus passing up immature bucks and allowing them to gain some age before being taken. On those ranges the hunters who spent time looking found shed antlers.

The possible exception to the above explanation for lack of shed antlers is an abundance of rodents and varmints -- mice, rats, rabbits and squirrels. These small creatures love to chew on deer antlers for the calcium, phosphorous and other minerals contained in them. However, I live in an area populated by a tremendous number of rodents and varmints, their numbers rivaling those anywhere, and still the shed antlers do not disappear that rapidly! Also, in some areas with extremely high rainfall rates, cast deer antlers have a tendency to disappear quite rapidly. Nonetheless, I still contend that a lack of shed antlers indicates a lack of mature bucks within the area.

An interesting fact about sheds: The longevity of shed antlers depends upon many factors. Exposure to rain and sun can break them down fairly quickly (two to three years) in some areas. In other regions that are relatively arid, shed antlers may last ten or more years.

What shed antlers reveal about bucks

Shed antlers also can teach us something about the size or potential size of the buck which cast them, as well as something about his age. In most instances small antlers belong to relatively young bucks and larger sheds belong to relatively older bucks. This is only natural. However, we can get a good idea of a buck's age by comparing the antlers' pedicel attachment area to the size of the main beam just above the burr.

As mentioned, with a young buck the shed antler is going to be relatively small. The pedicel attachment area is small and the size of the beam just above the burr also is small. In some bucks with

The late winter or even during the spring turkey season is an ideal time to scout, such as Greg Simons is doing here. Sheds can provide much information about a buck and be the key to finding him later.

extremely good potential for big antlers, the antler might be relatively small in main beam length, tine length, points and even mass. The pedicel attachment area, however, might be fairly large in comparison to the small antler above the burr. A buck that sheds such an antler bears watching and hunting in the future.

As bucks get to be two or three years old, the overall size of the antler increases in size. The sizes of the antler just above the burr and the pedicel attachment area, are nearly equal in size in these age classes.

Should you find a sizeable shed antler with several points, good main beam and tine lengths, with good mass, could it be from a mature deer in his prime? Again a good way to tell is by comparing the size of the antler above the burr to the pedicel attachment area. If the deer is in his prime the shed will have a fairly large pedicel attachment, but the beam just above the burr will be larger than the attachment area. Such a deer generally is four, five or six years of age. However, in some areas a three-year-old might exhibit such characteristics, especially if the deer is on an extremely high-nutrition diet.

On a deer whose antler development is starting to decline primarily because of age, the pedicel attachment area will be large and the main beam just above the burr will be smaller than the attachment area. This is the case with many over the hill bucks. However, if the deer's diet is extremely high in nutritional value and highly palatable, the deer may not decrease in antler development or size until he reaches an extremely advanced age. Some deer never do seem to reach an age when they start declining in antler development.

Realize, of course, that these statements are generalities, possibly a rule of thumb. But, bear in mind that nearly all such rules are broken at one time or another.

During the years I intensively managed several properties for the best possible white-tailed bucks, I was able to find sheds from the same buck, year after year. Each year the size of the shed increased in size. Occasionally I saw the buck during the time he wore the antlers, sometimes when they were gone. My associates and I made great efforts to find the serially shed antlers. When we were not harvesting many bucks, I often used the antlers to gauge the progress of our bucks and our management program. The shed antlers therefore proved invaluable, even as management tools.

Shed antlers also are often the ultimate key to locating where to hunt big bucks. As mentioned, a shed reveals where a particular buck was at one point in his life. Why he was there may be a bit of a mystery, but chances are it was because he resided in close proximity to food, water and cover.

A shed antler often has led me to a particular buck. On numerous occasions, hunting partners and I have taken bucks within fewer than 400 yards of where we had found sheds from previous years. In several cases we have taken deer within 100 yards of where we had found sheds from the same buck -- the year previous.

Each time I find a shed antler, I make a rough sketch of it in my buck journal and note where it was found. In addition to marking the location on my primary map, I also draw a little map in the journal showing where the antler found, and possibly where it was found in relationship to other antlers -- including a shed found from the same buck in years past. Each shed serves as an integral piece to a much larger puzzle.

Keeping a journal of what you find can lead to bucks later in the fall.

Several years ago, Ron Porter (an ex-game warden from New Mexico and of my hunting partners of many years) and I found shed antlers from a particular buck during a late winter scouting trip combined with a wild hog hunt. The matched set of shed antlers had come from a huge 10 point. His longest tines were well over 14 inches, giving the antlers a modest 18-inch inside spread that exceeded the Boone & Crockett typical minimums. We hunted hard for the buck the next year but never saw him. Two years later I shot the buck. Interestingly, he was shot within 200 yards of where we had found the sheds.

Several miles to the east of that ranch I shot a buck fewer than 40 yards from where I had found his sheds from the previous year -- only a few months earlier. In another instance I shot an impressive eight-point within 75 yards of where I had found one of his sheds two years earlier. Then there was the buck with palmate antlers that was shot practically under the same tree where his sheds had been found three years earlier. Or, how about the time Nolan Ryan, the baseball great, shot a long-tined buck within 200 yards of where the buck's sheds had been found two years previous. Numerous other hunters to whom I have talked have had similar experiences. Simply coincidence? I seriously doubt it.

I truly enjoy hunting sheds during the off-season, and while it is fun, there certainly are many other reasons for doing it. I can appreciate the size of a shed antler, learn something about the buck, maybe even measure his progress -- if I have found a shed from the same buck in years previous. And, equally important, the shed might be the key to unlock the mystery of where the old buck lives.

Using shed antlers to determine mineral licks

As mentioned, rodents and varmints love to chew on cast deer antlers, but so do other critters, whether cows, deer, coyotes or almost any four-footed animal in the forest or field. Therefore, fairly fresh shed antlers that exhibit a considerable amount of chewing may indicate that the area is low in calcium, phosphorous, salt or other trace minerals. If this is the case, and if the practice is legal, consider establishing several "natural" salt or mineral licks. Before doing this, however, be sure to check with the local game warden to find out if you are allowed to put out minerals or salt for deer and other wildlife.

Some state game departments, unfortunately, view this procedure as wrong and illegal. I argue that if the deer and other animals in the area will benefit and be healthier, the authorities should give their blessing to salt and mineral licks. Thankfully, mineral supplementation licks are not illegal in every state or province. But always make sure it's legal before you do it.

Some managers prefer mineral blocks. In my experience, I have had far better success and utilization by using loose mineral, primarily a mixture containing 12 percent phosphorous and 12 percent calcium, along with a good trace mineral package. The amount of salt added to the mixture should depend upon whether or not the soil in your area contains a great deal of natural salt, or virtually none.

To establish a mineral lick, I train deer to come to a particular spot before setting up the mineral lick. To do this I dig a shallow hole, much wider than deep, and stock the hole with shelled corn. This will get deer to start coming to that location. After they start coming for corn, I pour the mineral mixture into the depression and throw a little corn on top. Once the deer have become accustomed to the presence of mineral I quit baiting the area with corn. After that I frequently freshen the mineral lick with more of the mixture. Again, I stress, before putting out any salt or mineral be sure the practice is completely legal! Also, I realize this is a management technique, but the need for minerals is discerned by paying attention to shed antlers.

The advantages of summer scouting

To me the ideal time to scout for the upcoming hunting season is during the summer. When the days are long and warm, deer often will spend time in the same areas where they will be found in the early part of the hunting season. This also is a time when deer pay little attention to people wandering in their habitat. On the other hand, if just before the hunting season a hunter spends too much time in the area he intends to hunt, it is not uncommon for mature bucks to change their habits. I have seen this occur numerous times on properties I have managed.

Before the hunting season opens, bucks often are seen with great regularity. But a couple of weeks before the season opens, the hunters start showing up, redoing hunting stands and blinds and spending a lot of time in the woods. As the hunters clear shooting lanes and leave their scent throughout the home range of the bucks, it seems the bucks realize this increase in human activities in their area spells upcoming trouble. Within a couple of days the bucks start changing their patterns. Instead of emerging from the brush to feed in the open areas, they enter those areas only after legal shooting hours. Next thing you know the mature bucks are changing their travel routes and the times at which they move to adjust to the human activities.

With this in mind, rather than spend time scouting either right before hunting season, or even during the season, a much better time to scout hunting country is during the summer. During this time deer do not seem to mind humans in their home areas. And, even if they did "mind" humans in their home ground, by the time hunting season comes along the deer will have forgotten about the disturbance.

Using rubs and scrapes to your advantage

The summer is an ideal time to locate rubs and scrapes without disturbing the deer in the area. During that time they will pay little attention if someone "messes" around their scrapes. Scrapes are relatively easy to find even during the summer. A good place to look for scrapes used the previous fall is along the edge of natural openings or fields, along pasture or logging roads, and not far from favored feeding areas. Look for a shallow depression with an overhanging limb. In most instances it will show signs of having been chewed upon the year previous.

Once each scrape is located I make note of it on the map and in my buck journal. If I can establish a pattern to the scrapes I will set up a tripod stand in the area between the scrapes, on the downwind side. Or I might hang a climbing stand in the area, enhancing the chance that they'll be there when I arrive at the property the night before the opening of hunting season.

The summer also is a good time to cut some lanes through thick brush. Deer, just as you and I, will choose the path of least resistance when walking through thick brush. Thus, you can often funnel deer to walk right past your stand, or even to your stand. If you were to cut such lanes a few days before the season opened, the deer would be suspicious of such lanes. In addition, by cutting the lanes early you will create fresh regrowth brush that deer like to eat. That, too, may draw deer to your summer cut lanes.

Scrapes can play an important role in hunting mature bucks, as some bucks return to use the same scrapes year after year. More about their role in deer hunting, as well as the role of rubs as well, is covered in the next chapter.

Rubs also are easily distinguishable during the summer, especially rubs that have been used by bucks for several years. Bucks make rubs for a variety of reasons. Some are merely rubs of convenience, meaning the bucks are taking out frustrations on the nearest available woody adversary. Others are rubs that will be visited many times throughout the breeding season.

Several things can be learned by looking closely at rubs, both during summer scouting trips and hunting season forays. Bucks tend to rub more on one side of a tree or sapling than on another. This is because they tend to rub more on the side from which they have approached the rub. This will

Bucks often rub on the same bush or tree year after year. Finding such rubs indicates the presence of bucks in an area, even if you find them in late winter.

give you some indication as to the direction the buck normally travels. Finding two such rubs, as on a rub line, will reinforce your opinion about the direction the buck travels on a normal basis.

Closely inspecting the surface of a rub can give some idea as to the texture of the buck's antlers. If the rub is smooth, chances are good the surface of the deer's antlers are smooth. If the rub's surface is pitted and grooved, then chances are equally good the buck's antlers may have non-typical points around the bases, or at least antlers with many little knobby pearlings.

If a rub has some broken or scarred limbs or underbrush beyond the primary rubbing surface, this can indicate the buck's width, as well as his tine length.

Again, as mentioned, some bucks return each year to rub on the same trees or shrubs, or at least in the same area. These signs can be found easily during the summer months and recorded in your buck journal for future reference.

Tracks and trails are other signs to look for during summer scouting trips. I already have mentioned how a deer sometimes can be channeled toward certain trails by cutting lanes, or even stacking brush, in order to force him toward you. This is best accomplished in the summer, so by the time hunting season arrives the deer are accustomed to the change and the travelway has become a natural path.

The advantages of summer scouting include getting a jump on where to hunt certain bucks early in the hunting season. Bucks tend to remain in their same summer patterns until the first few weeks of fall. More will be discussed later about turning those summer scouting trips into early season hunting success.

When scouting, I try to record as much information as possible in my buck journal, such as where shed antlers were found, last year's rub and scrape locations, trails which show heavy current and previous use, and where I expect to find deer forage and mast crops later in the early fall.

A technique I often have employed when hunting in locales heavy with mast trees -- and probably thus with squirrels -- is to set up in an area with a binocular or spotting scope to look for squirrels. Where squirrels are abundant, you also will find an abundance of mast, and likely deer. This technique also works well in the early fall when scouting from a distance.

Summer scouting can play an important role in your hunting for mature bucks. I believe it can spell the difference between success and failure.

Chapter 6

Rubs and Scrapes

Next to seeing a buck while hunting, finding rubs and scrapes are two of the most important kinds of deer sign you can find. Some people insist finding tracks is equally important, and to some extent they are important. In fact, some people have told me they can readily distinguish the difference between buck and doe tracks. I normally can't.

Bucks rub their antlers in the fall. Finding such rubs indicates the presence of bucks in the area. But rubs can also tell you much more.

In some areas bucks do tend to have large feet because they are much larger bodied and framed than does. Perhaps in those areas there might be the possibility of distinguishing buck tracks from does. In other areas bucks and does have similar sized hoofprints. The only way I ever have distinguished buck from doe tracks has been when they were standing in them!

The presence of rubs and scrapes, however, indicates the presence of bucks in an area -- any area. How frequently these buck signs appear depends considerably on the deer density and the herd composition (i.e. buck-to-doe ratio, and percentage of mature bucks within the herd).

Why do bucks make rubs?

Bucks start making rubs about the time the velvet dies and begins coming off the antlers. Velvet comes off regardless of whether or not a buck rubs it. However, rubbing hastens the removal process. As the velvet comes off in strips and pieces, it normally is eaten by the buck in his effort to conserve valuable nutrients.

Weishuhn examines a large rub, and believes the bigger the rub, generally the bigger the buck that made it.

Bucks start making scrapes about three weeks to a month before the first breeding activity taking place, which has been theorized as a breeding-related activity. Some researchers have proposed that does, as the fall breeding season approaches, release certain pheromones which trigger sexual activity in bucks. These researchers sometimes refer to this event as the "silent" estrus, which is thought to help promote synchronization between the male and female breeding season. According to some researchers the timing of this silent estrus may be altered by the nutritional condition, the quality and quantity of forage. If nutrition is wanting, the early silent estrus might be delayed. This, in turn, might affect the timing of when the first scrapes to appear. However, I also have seen bucks making scrapes in areas where there were no does!

Research has indicated that if a herd has a large number of mature bucks, there likely will be more rubs and scrapes than in an area where there are few mature bucks. These rubs and scrapes serve not only as visual signposts, but also as olfactory signals by which bucks mark various areas to help establish their dominance.

We are continuing to learn about whitetail behavior. When a buck rubs his forehead on a rub, he deposits an odor produced by his forehead's tubular apocrine sudoriferous glands. As the rut approaches, these glands become more active. This explains why a rub not only is a visual sign, but also a scent communicator. Researchers in the Southeast found these "scent communication posts" can cause does to be ready to breed when the bucks are.

Does the size of a rub indicate the size of a deer? There is conflicting research regarding whether or not big bucks make big rubs. One research group says big bucks make big rubs. Another researcher states big bucks make only small rubs. Remember when I stated that big bucks are as individual as you or I? Methinks, that might be the case with big bucks and their rubs.

I have observed huge bucks making huge rubs on big trees and on small trees, as well as on saplings that were merely twigs. I prefer to think big bucks tend to make and use big rubs. In other words, the bigger the rub the bigger the buck or bucks that made it. As a biologist I am uncertain as to the truth of this view. As a hunter, however, I will continue to believe big bucks make big

Skipper Bettis of the Sanctuary examines a rub, but rubs such as made on this tree are small by comparison to some found on the Sanctuary.

rubs. So believe what you wish to believe. Research groups on each side of the debate will be right at least part of the time.

I have seen bucks return for several years to the same trees or areas to rub. These rubs are obvious because they show both old rubbing scars and freshly rubbed surfaces. In areas with quite a few mature bucks I have seen numerous bucks rub on the same tree within minutes of each other. I have observed big mature bucks stand and watch other bucks of equal size -- and apparent status -- rub on "their" rub.

I also have seen bucks get into fights around both rubs and scrapes. Were they being protective of their scrapes or rubs, or fighting because they simply happened to be two aggressive bucks in the same place? I also have rattled up a considerable number of bucks -- both youngsters and mature bucks -- near scrapes. Why did they respond? Were they simply in the area, or were they responding in order to protect their area? Who knows for sure?

Ron Porter examines an active scrape.

Is it important that we know exactly why bucks make rubs? Well, perhaps to a point. Knowing why certainly helps us understand more about white-tailed buck behavior. But to me, more important is the fact that we know bucks make rubs each fall and that their presence indicates there are bucks in the area!

In every area bucks tend to prefer to rub on certain shrubs, saplings and trees. Though the reason for this is uncertain, this probably is because some trees produce sap that is highly aromatic. Some saplings and shrubs tend to be resilient, pushing back when a buck pushes against them.

The particular plants bucks rub determine, to some extent, the color of a buck's antlers. In some areas favorite rubbing trees and saplings tend to be pines, in other areas it is junipers, in other areas -- such as the Southwest -- it is various acacias. I also have seen bucks rub their antlers on prickly pear cactus, fence posts, power poles impregnated with creosote or other aromatic wood preservatives, steel posts and other items.

Earlier I mentioned several things you might be able to learn from rubs, either those found during the summer or when hunting during the fall. The observant hunter that looks for such sign throughout the year learns well!

Bucks, especially mature bucks, frequently check and freshen their scrapes. Most such activities take place at night.

Learning from scrapes

Scrapes, according to some researchers, are made to attract females for breeding and to intimidate rival males. Some observers believe most of the scrapes in an area are made by dominant bucks. Research conducted by Karl Miller, and reported in the pages of *Deer & Deer Hunting* by Rich Waite in 1992, suggests that high dominance rank may not be as important as the buck's physical and behavioral maturity. Waite also reported that bucks that have taken part in previous ruts produce significantly more scrapes than younger males.

Scrapes consist of pawed-out areas in the soil where the buck urinates, often urinating on his tarsal glands and letting the fluid trickle to the soil below. (However, some does have been seen making scrapes.) Nearly every scrape is made beneath an overhanging limb. The limb serves as a spot for the buck to leave his scent in the form of both saliva and secretions from his forehead glands. While does have been observed pawing the ground in scrapes and urinating in them, they never have been observed "working" the overhead limb.

Researcher John Ozoga reports that most of the scraping activity is done two weeks before the peak of the rut. After this intense period of scraping activities, the number of visitations declines daily. He also found, in the area where his research was conducted, that nearly 80 percent of all scrapes were made before the first female conceived. His research further showed that only 35 percent of all scrapes were visited by deer during a 24-hour period at the height of the rut. This makes one wonder if hunting right next to a scrape or scrape line is worthwhile during the peak of the rut.

While scrapes may be made by bucks and does, rubs are a sure sign of bucks in an area.

As with Waite's article, Ozoga also reported finding that 65 percent of the scrapes made the previous year were reopened the following year, and that 95 percent of these old scrapes contained deer tracks throughout the year. Some researchers suggest deer use the overhead branch of the scrape to scent-mark their territories throughout the year. Other researchers who keep tabs of such things tell me that approximately 75 percent of all scraping activity occurs after dark.

During the years I have had the opportunity to keep tabs on several scrapes that might be considered primary, breeding, active or whatever you choose to call them. My feeling is that a scrape is active as long as it is being used -- even if it lies untouched for months. I have seen some scrapes opened up, but then were never again visited. I also have watched scrapes that have been reopened each fall for at least six years. I recall one scrape I found soon after beginning work with the ranch. Six winters later, when I quit working with the ranch, the scrape still was active.

That scrape has been equally interesting for another reason. One fall as the rut approached, I sat in a blind near the scrape from daylight to dark. During the daylight hours 13 different bucks visited the scrape. Several of those bucks were mature, and several of them certainly could be considered dominant bucks, based on their large bodies and antlers. None of the daytime bucks appeared at the scrape at the same time, but each freshened the scrape. If 75 percent of bucks visit scrapes at night, this means three times more bucks probably used the same scrape after dark.

The area around this particular scrape -- and two others which were active nearly every fall -- was one of my favorite horn rattling areas. During the hunting season I seldom failed to rattle up one or more bucks in the area near the very active scrapes, including after the peak of the breeding season.

Mature buck during the rut have swelled necks, and legs that almost appear to be too short for their big bodies.

Research has shown that the best period to hunt scrapes is from the time the first scrapes appear until the rut starts to peak. I have seen numerous bucks work scrapes at all times of the day, from first light through the late afternoon. And more than once I have seen a buck walk to where he could see the scrape plainly, approaching it from downwind in order to smell it. If there seemed to be no reason to freshen the scrape, the buck simply stood watching for a while, then silently slipped back into the underbrush.

Obviously, you can learn a lot by just watching. Regardless of whose research you follow, or choose to believe, rubs and scrapes can play an important role in scouting for and taking a mature buck.

Chapter 7

As the Seconds Tick Away

The buck stood at the edge of the old logging road that cut through the woods. Only a small portion of his right antler, eye and ear were visible from behind an impenetrable wall of saplings and underbrush. I was amazed that any part of the buck was visible.

By all rights I should not have seen him. I had only because I'd been watching that exact spot when the deer appeared. All around me the southeastern pines, hardwoods, and tangles of briar and underbrush dripped with rain, muffling any footfalls. Had the forest floor been dry I might have heard the buck's approach, but instead he had moved silently over the soggy, leaf littered ground. The buck stood momentarily, and then turned and walked away. Just as quickly as he had appeared, he was gone. It was as if he had melted from sight without ever offering me the opportunity of a shot. In my estimation that is typical mature buck behavior. Had I placed my climbing tree stand in a pine on the opposite side of the road there might have been a chance at the buck.

While hunting in Canada the following year I spotted a buck as he momentarily stopped in a small clearing, just long enough to look my way. Before I could position my gun for a steady shot, especially at that long distance, he again disappeared.

I have had similar sightings of bucks from down in the *brasada* of Mexico to just below the tundra of Canada, and from the foothills of the Rocky Mountains to the Eastern Seaboard. In some of those brief encounters I have triumphed, but in far too many of I have ended up only wishing for a shot.

Big mature bucks are different than other deer. Such a buck seldom strikes a calendar pose that allows the hunter time to carefully study his antler attributes or even admire him. Seldom, if ever, does a big mature buck give the hunter more than five seconds to see him, evaluate him as to antler size and age, estimate the distance, and make a killing shot. That is less time than many people would take to read the last sentence. In other words, that is a brief period of time!

Hesitate and all is lost. Rush your decision and you might make the wrong one, not take the type of deer you desire, or -- even worse -- make a non-killing shot. However, if you expect a mature buck to give you more than five seconds to see and accomplish, you likely will return to camp muttering to yourself and your hunting partners about the big one that got away.

Learning to see deer

The first step in taking a regally antlered mature buck is to see him. That means hunting where such animals exist and where you will have a reasonable opportunity at a buck of this age. We already have discussed how to select a hunting area when seeking to take a mature buck.

Mature bucks seldom give the hunter more than five seconds to see them, evaluate them as to age and antlers, estimate distances, and make a killing shot.

In every camp one individual seems to have an almost extraordinary ability to see deer. Is there something magical about the guy, or does he have special powers? No, he probably is just observant. The first step to seeing deer is to *enter the woods with the right attitude.* If you think positively about seeing deer you likely will.

Far too many hunters head to the woods with thoughts of other than deer hunting on their minds. They may be thinking about problems at work, how to close a particular deal, or about financial or personal problems. True, the deer woods are excellent places to work out problems or think about things other than hunting. However, these matters are best pondered before entering or after leaving the deer woods.

While in the woods think positively of seeing deer and of hunting opportunities. In that way you will be mentally prepared when a mature deer presents himself. My dad used to exhort me when he dropped me off at my deer blind, "Remember, be awake!" In other words, don't daydream and be ready when you get a chance at a deer. If your mind is full of thoughts other than deer hunting, you may not notice slight movement amid the underbrush, or hear a hoof fall in the dry leaves.

As part of maintaining the right attitude, *expect to see deer when in the woods,* and you most certainly should. If none appear, you should be hunting in another area. But when in the deer woods, look for *pieces* of deer rather than full body poses.

I know what I am about to say may sound extremely basic to readers who are serious mature buck hunters. However, I think it important to be reminded occasionally about the basics. As stated above, look for *pieces* of deer -- watching for patches of brown hair where there should be greens and grays. Look for horizontal lines where there should be vertical. Look for the twitch of a tail or the wiggle of an ear. Look for the black spots, such as a deer's nose and eyes.

Look for the glint of sun reflecting from a buck's antler or his sleek coat. Several times I have zeroed in on a deer only because I could see a shiny black nose, or the sheen of his sleek hair. A fall fattened buck has an extremely sleek, almost "greasy" coat that reflects light when the sun shines on it. This often betrays the presence of a deer.

Often other forest or field animals, such as crows, ravens, jays and squirrels, betray the presence of a deer. These may sound off a warning long before you see the deer. When in the deer woods, therefore, pay attention to what goes on around you, not only with your eyes but with your ears -- and even your nose. Sometimes you can even smell the musky odor of a rutting buck.

Keep your eye on the head

As soon as you've spotted a deer, concentrate on its head. Doing this is paramount. During the past 20 years I have conducted a considerable number of helicopter game surveys, having flown surveys on well over 15 million acres. While so doing, I have taught myself to visually "pick up" deer by their movement and then to sweep past their bodies and concentrate on their heads to determine if they are bucks or does -- and then the size of their antlers.

This technique is not unlike that of a shotgun shooter who is extremely adept at shooting clay targets. When the clay target appears, he "picks it up," swings through for the proper lead and squeezes the trigger. If he simply watches the clay target or shoots without leading, in most all instances he will miss the target. The same concept works well when looking at deer. If you want to become good at determining whether a deer is a buck or a doe, you'll have to swing through the body and go for the lead, or in this instance the deer's head.

The first step always is to determine if the deer is a buck or a doe. If the deer lacks antlers, start looking around the doe or even elsewhere. If you concentrate too long on a particular animal you might miss another one that is moving within the area you are watching.

If you do see antlers, try to determine if both sides of the rack are present. If both are present, then try to determine the size of the buck's rack, in terms of number of points, tine length, main beam length, spread, and massiveness, and -- if you are interested in such things -- the buck's gross Boone & Crockett score.

Before going on each hunting trip, decide upon a minimum for the size buck you are hoping to take. In some instances this might be a buck with at least a certain number of points or spread, or even a minimum gross Boone and Crockett score, plus the fact the buck is a mature deer. My personal goals vary for each hunting trip and area. Some areas tend to produce extremely big and interesting antlers, others may produce mature bucks, but no particularly big antlers. If I am hunting in the brush country of south Texas, or in another area with a tendency to produce large-antlered mature bucks, I will set a minimum standard for the buck I am seeking. However, if I see a buck that doesn't quite meet one or more of my criteria, but far surpasses another, I likely will take him -- even though he is not "perfect."

I personally like bucks with racks that have massive beams and long tines. Spread is a minor concern to me, while someone else might be more interested in a wide rack. (One of the friends with whom I hunt frequently is enamored with wide spread bucks.) Your choice of a buck and rack might be one with lots of points. Or you, as some, may go bonkers over a buck whose rack has drop tines, which are rare everywhere.

As soon as I spot a deer, I look at his head and determine if he indeed has the kind of rack I am hoping to take. My minimum usually is a buck with eight points. I dearly love big eight-point bucks. I get both tickled and aggravated by hunting partners who return to camp with ashen complexions, still shaking, and mumbling something about having just seen the biggest buck in their life. When questioned about the deer and asked if they got a shot, they will reply, "He was the biggest deer I have ever seen, wide, tall and heavy! But I didn't shoot at him because he was just an eight point..."

Where most bucks are harvested at a young age, such as this buck, there will be little chance of finding mature bucks.

To me, that reaction is not very smart. A monster buck is a monster buck, and one with eight points that accumulates many inches of measurements as an eight point is much more impressive than one that does it as a 10 or more point buck. My highest scoring typical white-tailed buck is a huge eight point and he is considerably more impressive than several multi-pointed bucks that nearly equal his score.

I follow the eight point minimum because most bucks with fewer than eight points are likely to be younger deer. However, if deer are enjoying a good level of nutrition, even yearling bucks (those 14 to 18 months of age) may develop eight or more points during their first antler year.

In looking at a buck's rack I strive to see if both sides are present. If the buck has a main beam, and two primary tines and brow tine on either side of his rack, he will be at least an eight point. If he has brow tines and three tines rising off either main beam, he will be a 10 point buck. If he has four points and a brow tine on each main beam, the buck should be a typical 12 point. If he has five primary tines and a brow tine, he will be a typical 14 point. The number of bucks seen beyond the typical 10 point count will be extremely few.

I have shot one typical 13 point, an old 6 by 7 buck, but I have yet to take a typical 12 point (though several hunting companions have shot a number of these). I have hunted in some of the best deer country in North America for many years, and have had only one chance at a typical 12 point, a buck we rattled up. Unfortunately, I got overly excited about the deer and missed -- with him standing nearly at the end of my rifle barrel. Sometimes even when nearly everything is done right, a spent rifle case is all that remains by which to remember a particularly large buck.

Taking a typical 12 point buck actually is one of my personal hunting goals. I have shot a great number of typical 11s. Hopefully there will be a typical 12 in my future. Not only have I hunted some extremely good country, I have had the opportunity to observe hundreds of thousands of white-tailed bucks while conducting game surveys. Those bucks with 12 typical points are extremely rare, even in the best of deer country.

As for typical 14 point bucks, I have seen only four such live deer in a lifetime of hunting and working as a biologist. Two of those bucks later were shot -- the taking of one of them is described later in this book.

Non-typical bucks with many points tend to excite most people. Such bucks also are quite rare and generally are shot whenever seen, without much time taken to evaluate them. I would do the same, were I so fortunate to see one! I have seen few bucks with huge non-typical racks.

From a distance my best non-typical looks like a giant eight point with long tines, but in fact has 24 points well over an inch long, with several more nearly an inch long. He was one of those bucks which grew larger, the closer I got to him. Some times such points are "hidden" on the backside of the rack or are bunched around the bases.

Estimating rack size at a distance

To estimate the relative size or length of a buck's tines, main beam, spread and massiveness, there are several body comparisons you can use to determine quickly these measurements and the buck's gross Boone & Crockett score.

The primary contributors to that accumulative gross Boone and Crockett score are main beam length and tine length. Inside spread is a secondary contributor. To determine tine length consider that most white-tailed bucks' ears measure about 8 inches from the tip to where they attach to the head. The inside opening of a deer's ears is about 6 inches in length. Use these dimensions, or multiples thereof, to determine the length of the antler tines.

Another good comparison measurement is the same one taxidermists use to determine the proper form for your mount -- the eye to nose measurement. This is measured from the forward tip of the nose to the forward tip of the eye. This measurement varies somewhat from region to region. For example, big Northern bucks might measure as long as 8 inches, while Southern bucks may range from 6 to 7 inches.

As I've already emphasized, do your homework before hunting. Call a local taxidermist and ask for the average measurements of local deer, including the eye to nose distance and the length of deer's ears, as well as their ear tip to ear tip measurement when a deer's ears are held in an erect and forward position. In most instances, the average eye to nose measurement is 7 inches. Ear tip to ear tip measurements vary significantly.

Most big northern deer have an eye to nose measurement of seven to eight inches, and ear lengths of 8 inches. Using these can quickly help you estimate antler sizes.

Tine length

Suppose you have spotted a buck with five points per side and a total of 10 obvious typical points. His brow tines are about half as long as his entire ear, or about 4 inches. His first primary (or back) tine is about one and a half times as long as his ear, or about 12 (8 + 4) inches in length. The next forward primary tine is of approximately equal length to his ear or about 8 inches. His third primary tine, moving forward, is about half as long as his eye to nose measurement or about 3 inches. Thus far, his accumulated tine length on one side totals 27 inches (4 + 12 + 8 + 3 = 27).

Main beam length

The gross Boone & Crockett score is an accumulation of total tine lengths, main beam lengths, and four circumferences on both sides of the rack, plus the inside spread. The next objective is to determine the length of the main beam. For this use either the eye to nose measurement or the length of the ear measurement (actually multiples of those markers). Let's say the main beam appears to be almost three times the length of the ear, but a little more than three times the length of the eye to nose measurement. Thus the main beam measures about 22 inches.

Circumference

To estimate the circumference, assume that the average whitetail eye is approximately 1 inch in diameter and approximately 4-1/2 inches in circumference. So let's assume the first measurement taken between the burr and the brow tine is about the same diameter as the eye, or about 4-1/2 inches. The next measurement between the brow tine and the back tine is approximately the same size. The third measurement, taken between the first and second primary tine, is only slightly smaller or about 4 inches. The last measurement, taken between the second and third primary tines, is about the same. This yields a total of 17 inches of mass or circumference measurements (4-1/2 + 4 1/2 + 4 + 4 = 17). Had the deer been an eight point, the fourth circumference estimate would have been taken halfway between the end of the main beam and the most forward tine.

To complete the score of the one side, add the total tine length to the main beam length to the four circumferences (27 + 22 + 17 = 66) for a total measurement of 66 inches on one side. Now simply double the 66 score, since both sides are approximately equal, and the antler score thus far is 132. To this you should add the inside spread estimate.

Inside spread

Ear tip to ear tip measurements average from about 14 to 17 inches, depending upon the area you hunt. In this instance let us say you are hunting an area where the average deer weighs about

200 pounds (live weight) and has an ear tip to ear tip spread of about 16 inches. When the buck looks your way with his ears held in an erect position, you notice his antlers are spread right to the edge of those ears, giving him an approximately 16-inch inside spread. You then complete your estimate of the gross Boone & Crockett score by adding antler measurements from each side of the rack to the inside spread dimension for a total of 148 B&C points (66 + 66 + 16 = 148).

The best way to practice estimating Boone & Crockett gross scores is to spend time with mounted deer heads. Look at each one very briefly and estimate number of points, tine lengths, main beam lengths, circumference and inside spread to obtain your gross score estimate. Then take the actual measurements to see how close your estimate was. After doing this many times you will almost automatically get an impression of the rack and what it scores. You will be surprised at how closely you can estimate scores with just a first and quick impression. But it must be quick if you wish to take big bucks.

The average buck's eye is approximately one inch in diameter and 4 1/2 inches in circumference. Knowing this you can quickly estimate the buck's circumference measurements of his main beams.

When hunting where numerous mature bucks exist, you very well may and should have opportunities at one or more sizeable deer. When you see such a buck quickly check to see if most of the points are present and have not been broken, or that one entire main beam is not gone. Broken tines and beams are not uncommon in areas with many mature bucks.

A few years ago I got a quick profile look at a buck whose nearest antler appeared as a wall of points. I hastily counted no fewer than 10 points on the nearest side. With great excitement I prepared to squeeze the trigger. Then I looked past the side of the rack closest to me. The other side of his rack was gone, its bright white color revealing it had been broken only a short time. I pushed the safety back on and simply admired the buck, wondering what the other buck might have looked like. Obviously a buck big enough to snap off the massive main beam of this buck had to be special.

Unless such things do not concern you, always make sure both sides of the rack are present, as are most of the tines. I felt assured the multi-tined buck would have a complete rack again the next year. He did and was taken by an old friend, making me doubly glad I'd passed up the broken rack.

All this observation and calculation within fewer than five seconds - and we've only spotted the buck and estimated his points and Boone & Crockett score. We still have not decided whether or not he is mature, how far away he is or if we can make a killing shot. The seconds tick away and valuable few remain.

Estimating a buck's age

In earlier chapters I have stated deer are individuals very much as you and I are. And just as you and I they age with the passage of time. In estimating the ages of deer we can compare them to relative age classes of humans. Young, year-ling and two-year-old bucks look like gangly teenagers. A deer of this class moves with certain speed and agility, though it has not yet matured to full stature and muscle development. The skin about its face and neck is tight, its belly line straight. During the breeding season its neck does not swell, or at best only slightly. Unless it is the only breeding male in the herd its hocks or tar- sals are relatively clean during the rut.

By the time a buck be- comes a three-year-old his body has begun to fill out, his muscles becom- ing fully developed. He is, however, still relatively slim with fairly straight lines. During the fall

Some mature bucks never develop large antlers, but that does not mean they will not be challenging to hunt.

breeding season his neck will swell to at least the points of his jaws -- his lower jaws where the head attaches to the neck -- and often past them. His skin still is tight about his face and neck. His hocks may be stained dark during the rut. The buck is an active participant of the rut and is constantly on the move.

The mature four and five year old deer can be compared to a 40 year old man. He is starting to put on a little weight. His belly line sags a bit. Though during the rut he may have a large swelled neck, the skin about his neck and face is starting to sag a bit. He has begun to develop jowls, loose flaps of skin hanging beneath his lower jaw. He moves a bit more slowly than before. His hocks during the rut are stained dark all the way to his ankles. From a distance he appears to be mostly neck, shoulder and midsection.

A buck that lives beyond the five year old class tend to look like an old man. His face has an abundance of loose skin about it and his face sags, complete with jowls. His once trim belly line now sags, and no longer does he move with the same grace he did when younger. From a distance his body appears too big for his legs. He looks almost "short-legged." He may have a huge neck and dark hocks, or he may not.

A buck that is "over the hill" may, at first glance from a distance, look like a younger bucks except for his great antlers. And until you take a closer look at his slack face and pot belly he may appear to be younger, since he shows no sign of a swollen neck.

If you are seeking a mature deer do you know what to look for? My best advice is to compare that deer to a late 40 or early 50 year old human male. If the buck looks the part, you are looking at a mature buck.

Far too many hunters have never seen a mature whitetail, but as more hunters and hunting groups strive for quality management the incidence of mature buck sightings surely will rise.

Estimating range

As the seconds tick away you have decided the buck is a 10 point that will gross score close to 150 Boone & Crockett points, and that he is probably four or five years old -- supposedly in his prime antler development years. You make the decision to take him, but how far away is he? Is he within your range, regardless of what you are shooting?

There are several ways to estimate range. One way is to step off the distances from your blind to various landmarks before the deer arrives. In some areas estimating the distance is no problem, because the greatest distance you can shoot seems to be 100 yards or less. Right? Maybe not.

When hunting among pines where there are clearcuts you might be surprised at how far you can shoot. The same is true wherever there are fields, or powerline right of ways. The longest shot I've made on a white-tailed buck occurred in southern Georgia where most hunters tell me they never shoot over a hundred yards. In this instance the shot was over 500 yards. Had I not known how to estimate the distance or where to hold for such a shot the opportunity would have been lost. But I knew how to use scope as a range estimator. I had practiced many times at that distance and knew where to hold, relative to the distance.

To estimate distances I use my variable (3.5X to 10X) scope with duplex crosshairs. Normally I leave the scope power set on 5X. At 100 yards the average deer, which is about 40 inches in length from the

It is imperative to be thoroughly knowlegedgeable of your rifle, its capabilities and your capabilities as well.

forward tip of his brisket to the backside of his hindquarters, is bracketed between the broad portions of the horizontal crosshairs. In this way, if a deer is bracketed by the broad portion of the crosshairs, or appears even larger, I immediately know the buck is within 100 yards.

This method is equally important whether hunting with a modern rifle, a muzzleloader (check your state regulations to determine whether or not it is legal to use a scope with magnification on a muzzleloader while hunting deer) or a shotgun (again check local regulations). A modern muzzleloading rifle or shotgun with modern slugs is capable of cleanly killing deer at ranges out to 100 yards.

With my Simmons scope a deer 300 yards away is bracketed by the broad portion of the crosshairs at a power setting of eight. At 400 yards the same is true with a power setting of between 9 and 10. But generally, I leave the power adjustment of my scopes set on five. If the deer is a long distance away, I normally have enough time to crank up the power on the scope.

While some scopes have a built-in range finder with extra lines in the scope, I find these somewhat confusing, especially when I am excited about the possibility of taking a big deer. Under those circumstances I want things to be as simple as possible. I want nothing extra to confuse me.

Using a rest

At this point you have made a decision to shoot the buck you've been analyzing. You have estimated the distance -- in this case just a little over 100 yards. Of the five seconds the buck will give you to decide and shoot, you have spent the great majority determining that he is a mature deer with the antler development you desire to take. You have determined the distance -- one at which both the rifle and you are capable and proficient.

Normally a hundred-yard shot is one which the shooter should make off-hand. However, the sight of the big buck may have given you a slight case of the buck fever. (they affect me that way.) You are trembling with excitement. Should you try an off-hand shot or find a rest from which to steady your shot?

All of us who hunt mature whitetails are the world's best marksmen. But it is amazing how many of us miss easy shots. It happens, especially when shooting off-hand and at a big deer. For that reason, if at all possible I shoot from a solid rest. While hunting, therefore, I spend half my time looking for deer and the other half looking for a solid rest from which to shoot. This is especially true when not

Good optics and a steady rest are important when there is little time to evaluate a buck.

hunting from a blind or stand. If I am hunting where I doubt there will be any solid rests available, I carry one of several crossed shooting sticks. These are light-weight, easily carried and quickly available when I need them. Having them available has helped me make many shots, both close and long range.

Aiming at the right spot

Now comes the question of where is the best place to shoot the buck. This depends considerably on his angle, the direction in which he is facing. Numerous hunters have told me they advocate neck shots because they believe a neck shot will either kill or miss. I strongly disagree with such logic, for I have seen several big bucks get wounded and escape because they were shot through the neck.

During the rut a mature buck has a large, swelled neck, and the spine is small. The enlarged neck, of course, distorts the location of the spine. If the shot misses the spine the deer likely will get away, wounded. And that is the last thing you want to do to a magnificent white-tailed buck. Merely wound him with such shot to the neck and you will never see him again. I therefore do not believe in shooting a mature buck in the neck. Doing so greatly diminishes your chances of killing cleanly, quickly and humanely, all which I believe we owe to any animal we hunt and take.

When hunting a mature deer I strive to place my bullet through the deer's shoulders, breaking them and hopefully doing great injury to his spine or lungs. Given the opportunity I will shoot a buck about a third of the way down from the top of his withers to the bottom of his brisket. Such a shot will break both shoulders and likely will strike the spine as well.

On a forward quartering shot I will do my best to place the bullet into the forward shoulder and angle it through the lungs. With an opposite shot, in this case the deer quartering away from me, I will try to shoot so the bullet will pass through the opposite, off-side shoulder, breaking it and doing considerable damage to the lungs.

If the deer is facing me, I will try to place the bullet so it will pass through the lung area, holding just about where the neck portion of the spine meets the rest of the body. Such a shot will do damage to the top part of the lungs and also will likely do great damage to the liver. In this instance, if hit properly, the deer likely will not go far but he may leave only a small blood trail -- and possibly none at all.

Most of us, when hunting, will see a big buck walking directly away from us. View this buck prudently. Most bucks, regardless of their antler size and dimensions, always look much larger from the rear.

If presented with such a shot what should you do? Should you wait momentarily and hope he eventually stops and turns broadside, or offers a quartering shot? Or should you shoot him straight up the backside, hoping to hit at the base of his tail? If you hunt big deer this is a decision you likely will have to make sometime. I intend not to sway you either way, but consider my experiences.

During the years of collecting deer for research purposes I occasionally had to shoot a deer we particularly needed as it walked away from me. Those shot so the bullet struck at the base of the tail always went down immediately. And by the time I had walked the short or long distance to them, they were dead. I have seen others shoot deer going directly away from them, but the animals were merely wounded, and were not found in time to recover the meat. This occurred because the shot was too low, or because the deer was shot in the hindquarter in a non-fatal area.

Most of the shots I recommend might be viewed by some as destroying too much meat. Granted, an expanding bullet will render some meat unsuitable for human consumption. However, the shots I advocate will nearly always put the animal down either at the shot or only a few steps beyond. I would rather feed some trimmings to my dog than to shoot the deer in a different way and risk not finding the animal until all the meat has spoiled.

Decisions to take a buck, quite often come down to a matter of heartbeats. A split-second decision was required of the author in this instance.

The five-second decision

We've just spend a lot of time covering the tremendous amount of things that must be done in fewer than five seconds! Knowing how to get them done takes experience, and learning from mistakes -- even after years of experience. There is nothing wrong with making mistakes, as long as you learn and benefit from them in the future.

Neither is there anything wrong with occasionally missing a deer. It happens. If it has not yet happened to you, especially when shooting at a buck of your dreams, it likely will. I have missed sev-

Mature bucks seldom venture from cover, when they do you had better take full advantage of the situation. Seldom will a buck such as this give you more than 5 seconds.

eral good bucks. To my embarrassment, I even have done so in front of at least a couple of television cameras. And the shows were played on national television. Sure I regret those misses, but it happens!

How and what you do during the five seconds a big buck might-- I repeat, *might* -- give you will determine whether or not you hang your license tag on him. With time and repetition much of what we discussed in this chapter will happen automatically. One look and you will know he is mature, how many points he has, how wide he is, how tall are his tines, how wide is his spread and how massive are his beams. You'll immediately know how far he is and where to hold and where to place your shot from a predetermined solid rest. Well, maybe almost.

Chapter 8

Guns and Optics

Mature white-tailed deer come in all different sizes, from the diminutive Carmen Mountains whitetails and Coues whitetails of the Southwest, to the monstrous-bodied whitetails of the Dakotas and Northern woodland whitetails of the North Country. I have been fortunate to have hunted both ends of the size spectrum.

My smallest mature and fully developed whitetail was one of the Carmen Mountain subspecies. Taken in the high desert mountain country of Coahuila, Mexico, the five-year-old buck, with an impressive rack for his size, weighed 70 pounds (live weight). On the other end of the scale, my heaviest whitetail was a six year old, massive beamed buck taken in northern Michigan on the famed Sanctuary. That buck pulled the scale down to just over 300 pounds (live weight).

If there is something such as an "average" mature whitetail, it probably is one that weighs in the neighborhood of 200 to 225 pounds, and field-dresses at about 100 to 160 pounds. Mind you, I said mature, and not just the average white-tailed buck.

For the most part, in one respect, deer are fairly fragile. They are rather thin-skinned and boned. Yet in another respect, they are extremely tenacious and if not hit properly the first time, they can be extremely hard to bring down. This is especially true of big-bodied mature whitetails. When hunting such deer it is wise to use a highly accurate and hard-hitting firearm. In other words, "use enough gun."

GUNS

"Enough gun?"

The ideal combination of a deer rifle, caliber, cartridge and load is somewhat a personal choice, as is the action used. Some hunters prefer lever actions, others bolt actions, and still others semi-automatics and single shots. Some hunters claim to use semi-autos because such actions allow for fast follow-up shots. I, however, contend that if the first shot is properly placed there is no reason for a quick follow-up shot. I see no reason for using such actions when hunting deer. Potentially both of these types of actions are extremely accurate and strong.

What makes for an ideal whitetail cartridge? At the risk of making quite a few people mad at me, I believe that deer should not be hunted with anything less than the .25 calibers, beginning with the .257 Roberts and .250 Savage. This view excludes the .243 Winchester, the 6mm Remington and the like. In so saying I admit to having taken several deer with 6mm caliber rifles, and have seen several other deer taken with the .243 Winchester and similar calibers. But, I also have shot deer with everything from the diminutive .17 caliber to the .50 caliber.

For many years the lever action reigned supreme.

Just because deer can be killed with a caliber does not make it an ideal deer cartridge. In my opinion, the .243 Winchester belongs only in the hands of an expert who knows the limitations of the cartridge and, most certainly, his own skill.

I do not care for the 6mm cartridges because I have seen several deer wounded (by hunting clients) with them and not immediately recovered. In several of those cases the deer were properly hit in the vitals with a well-constructed bullet. Had I witnessed better experiences with the cartridges I might feel differently.

In my opinion, far better selections are the two .25 calibers already mentioned; the .270 Winchester; and the various 7mm cartridges from the ancient 7x57, to the .280 Remington, to the 7mm-08 Remington, and a multitude of other chamberings.

While I am not a supporter of the small calibers, neither am I necessarily a proponent of the super magnum calibers and cartridges. For the most part these are unnecessarily powerful. However, they are appropriate in situations where shots tend to be long. Some hunters think the magnum cartridge's greater velocity and downrange energy will allow them to kill a deer with nearly any kind of bullet placement, good or bad. That is certainly not the case! Nor

91

should this ever be assumed. Proper bullet placement still is paramount.

Another negative factor of larger magnum cartridges is their usually considerable recoil. For that reason some hunters do not shoot them very well. While the recoil can be lessened by porting the rifle barrel, this greatly increases the noise of a shot. However, if you like the hard hitting and long-range capabilities of the magnums, and if you can shoot them accurately, use them. I have used several and likely will again do so in the future. The magnums I have used most often when hunting deer are the 7mm Weatherby Magnum in a Weatherby Mark V, and the .338 Winchester Magnum in a Thompson/Center TCR'87 single-shot rifle.

My personal choice for an ideal whitetail cartridge is the .280 Remington in a bolt action or single shot rifle. I have owned several which were extremely accurate, and they have helped me account for numerous big, mature whitetails.

Bullet construction

Bullet construction and placement generally are more important than the size of a bullet's diameter. Shot placement, as mentioned earlier, is still paramount, because there are limitations with the bullets used for whitetails. Bullets, such as several of the ultra-fast varmint type that destruct upon impact have no place in deer hunting. Select a bullet that is extremely accurate, but also one that will penetrate and do most of its damage in the body cavity.

Also important are a bullet's velocity and down-range energy. Speed helps kill quickly by creating greater hydrostatic shock. When shooting a deer I want a well-constructed bullet that, upon entering the body, is traveling at sufficient speed. Once in the body the bullet needs to mushroom, increasing its overall diameter several times the original diameter, causing major tissue and bone damage before exiting the other side. Such a bullet will kill quickly, humanely, and efficiently. It also will leave a blood trail if the animal moves after being shot, making the recovery of the animal much easier.

Whether shooting a handgun such as the author or a rifle, take advantage of whatever rest you can.

Some hunters want a bullet that does not exit, and instead prefer one that delivers and expends all its speed and energy within the body of the deer. I have found merit in each kind of bullet. In most instances, the modern hunting bullet that exits has expended the vast majority of its energy within the cavity of the deer.

Mature bucks generally are big and tough and can take a lot of "putting down." If they lived on open plains with few hiding places, a wounded buck could be followed easily. However, big bucks generally live where there is considerable brush and underbrush, and often where the ground is hard and resistant to hoofprints -- making tracking difficult. Under such circumstances I prefer having a blood trail to follow if the deer does not go down immediately.

Caliber, cartridge and bullet selection are of extreme importance. Here from the smallest to the largest are some of the author's choices for rifles: 7mm-08 Remington, 7X57 Mauser, .280 Remington, 7mm Remington Magnum, 7mm Weatherby Magnum, and the 7mm Shooting Times Westener.

While bullet performance and shot placement are critical, so is the amount of energy the projectile delivers at the point of impact. Many cartridges and loads produce a fair to great amount of down-range energy. For it to be considered adequate as a deer cartridge, people who have conducted research in such matters believe a bullet should deliver no less than 1,000 foot pounds of down-range energy at the point of impact. At the point where the bullet no longer delivers that sort of energy, it should no longer be considered a worthy deer cartridge. This standard was established back in the days of Colonel Townsend Whelen. After years of adhering to the simple 1,000 foot pounds of energy rule, I cannot say I disagree!

By this rule a cartridge such as the .30-30 Winchester ceases to be a deer round at just under 200 yards. In contrast, the .270 Winchester using a 130 grain bullet produces better than 1,300 foot pounds of energy at 400 yards. The .280 Remington, .30-06 Government and like produce similar down-range energy at the same distance. Charts showing this data are available from most of the ammunition manufacturers, and also may be found in the annual *Deer Hunters' Almanac* from Krause Publications.

Before the bow hunters rise up in arms, let me say I realize that broadheads and arrow shafts do not even come close to delivering such down-range energy. Instead, sharp broadheads kill by cutting and hemorrhaging, rather than by hydrostatic shock. The two should not be compared. And be assured I have nothing against people who hunt with archery equipment. I have done a fair amount of bow hunting and truly enjoy it.

But personally, I enjoy hunting whitetail and other deer with rifles, handguns, muzzleloaders and even shotguns. I love the smell of gunpowder. To me, it is one of the most alluring perfumes! Please realize, therefore, I simply prefer to hunt with firearms. I know their capabilities, and my own, and have great confidence in them to quickly and humanely kill a deer, regardless of whether the distance is short or long.

Hunting handguns

Having already stated my personal minimums for rifles, I will do the same for handguns. In my opinion, the minimum handgun caliber which should be used for deer is the .41 Remington Magnum, though it is marginally adequate. I do not believe the .357 Magnum should be used on deer, and often have stated so in print. I realize that each year several deer are taken with the cartridge, and more probably will be taken in the future. In fact, I have shot several whitetail does with the .357 Magnum. Realistically, this is a handgun round better used for self-defense. It was not designed for hunting deer.

If I intend to hunt with a revolver, my preference is a .44 Rem Mag using at least 185 grain jacketed hollow point bullets that are extremely accurate in my two favorite hunting revolvers, the Ruger Super Blackhawk Hunter or Wesson with an eight inch barrel, which ever I happen to be hunting with at the moment. Some of the best hunting bullets and loads I have found for the .44 Rem Mag are the PMC Starfire and the custom loadings of Randy Garrett of Chelalis, Washington.

I do not consider even a .44 Magnum a suitable handgun deer cartridge beyond a range of 75 yards. After that point its down-range energy starts dropping off drastically. But if you enjoy getting close to the animals you hunt, are capable of doing so, and you like hunting with a revolver, the .44 Rem Mag should be your choice as well.

My personal handgun hunting favorites are the Thompson/Center Contender single-shot chambered for the .375 Winchester, or a Contender with a custom .309 JDJ barrel built by SSK Industries.

Wesson's .44 Rem Mag revolver is an excellent whitetail handgun, especially when combined with a Simmons handgun scope. However, by no means is this a long range combination.

One of the author's favorite handguns is the Ruger Super Blackhawk Hunter, complete with Simmons handgun scope. Note the shooting glasses worn by Bret Triplett; amber lenses provide great contrast.

I have used both of these, topped with a Simmons 2.5 by 7X handgun scope, with great success.

The .309 JDJ is my favorite for most circumstances. It was my choice when taking my highest scoring typical whitetail, as well as my heaviest buck. The latter weighed over 300 pounds and was shot at a distance of 125 yards. My 150 Nosler Ballistic Tip bullet hit the buck squarely just behind the shoulder. The bullet did considerable damage to the heart and lung area, then exited the opposite side. After only a few short steps the buck went down.

Other excellent handgun hunting calibers are the .30-30 Winchester; 7-30 Waters; .35 Remington; and .45-70 Government; as well as the 7mm-08 Remington and such wildcats as the 6.5 JDJ; 7 JDJ; .338 JDJ; and .375 JDJ. The latter, developed by J.D. Jones, one of the true handgun hunting experts, are available through SSK Industries in Wintersville, Ohio. All calibers mentioned are capable of cleanly taking even the largest of white-tailed deer. But even with these you must know their capabilities and your own at varying distance. Equally important, you must know you can place a bullet in the exact spot you want to hit. After that it is up to the bullet to do its job.

In my opinion a good hunting bullet should do considerable damage to internal tissue and bones before exiting the opposite side. I appreciate and enjoy looking at spent bullets that have done their job. Unfortunately, in order for a bullet to be recovered it must lodge in the body, rather than exit.

Bullet accuracy

Not only do bullets have to do a thorough job upon impact, they also have to be extremely accurate. Deciding which is more important is sort of a chicken or the egg question. Actually impact and accuracy are equally important.

But what constitutes accuracy? The average hunter likely is happy with his "hunting accuracy" if he can keep most of his shots within a dinner plate-sized circle at a distance of 100 yards. After all, a dinner plate pretty well corresponds with the approximate size of a deer's lung and heart area. While this might work for some, I want a little more accuracy. To me, hunting accuracy should be more precise than a 10-inch group at 100 yards. And the calibers and rounds I have come to prefer have served me well for several years, in many types of deer country.

Some experts claim hunting accuracy begins with groups no wider than two inches; others prefer groups no wider than 1-1/2 inches (both shot at 100 yards). My personal preference is for a rifle that shoots essentially same-hole accuracy at 100 yards, and extremely tight groups at 200 and even 300 yards. With such a rifle I know I can precisely place a bullet through a small opening, or slip a bullet between a couple of tree limbs to hit a big buck. My hunting rifles all shoot smaller than one inch groups. Sometimes I've had to do a bit of looking and hand loading to find ammunition or loads to do so. However, if I cannot get that kind of accuracy, the rifle soon will belong to someone else.

With my revolvers, I expect 2-inch or smaller groups at 50 yards. And I expect no greater than 1-1/2-inch groups with the rifle cartridge single-shot handguns I shoot -- primarily various Thompson/Center Contenders and Remington XP 100 single-shots. The .309 JDJ Contender I use often when hunting easily shoots less than 1-inch groups at 100 yards, using Nosler Ballistic Tip bullets.

I doubt there is a topic more frequently discussed in deer camps than the choice of firearms. I well remember back in the late 1950s, sitting around an old wood stove or an open campfire while listening to the merits of various deer rifles. Most of the discussion dealt with the various chambering for the Winchester Model 94 and the Savage Model 99, both lever actions. Back then in our area of Texas the lever action was king, as were the .30-30 Winchester and the .300 Savage. In time the discussions in those same camps changed to the .270 Winchester, the .30-06 Springfield, then later the .308 Winchester and the various magnums that hit the market. As a youngster I could cite the latest figures for each deer cartridge's velocity at varying ranges, and its down-range energy. I studied these statistics with the same zeal that others my age studied baseball batting records.

Since those days, radical changes have occurred in firearms, or at least so it seems. Thankfully, we have seen a return to the classic straight stock designs, which not only are good looking, but extremely functional as well. We also have seen a switch from traditional, beautifully grained wood stocks to much more functional synthetic stocks. While not as pretty by any means, they certainly are more durable and less vulnerable to changes in humidity that lead to warpage.

The muzzleloaders of today, such as Modern Muzzle Loading's MK-85, Thompson/Center's Thunderbolt and similar in-line muzzle loading rifles, are extremely accurate, especially when equipped with scopes and using loads that employ bullets encased in sabots. These are capable of extremely fine accuracy to distances of 100 or more yards.

The same can be said of slug barreled shotguns. With highly accurate and hard-hitting slugs encased in sabots, these new slug shotguns are capable of cleanly taking a deer out to 100 yards and beyond.

Both these types of firearms are becoming increasingly popular, not only because of their accuracy, but also because many states now are requiring shotguns or muzzleloaders, rather than rifles, when hunting deer. I suspect in the future, unfortunately, we will see more such regulations imposed as human populations continue to increase.

Becoming proficient

Regardless of your choice of firearms or archery equipment for hunting deer, it is important to be highly proficient with those choices. This requires many hours of practice, not only at the bench but also in the field. Finding a place to shoot, of course, is becoming increasingly more difficult. While ranges are available it often is nearly impossible to find a place to shoot at long-range silhouette targets, which teach not only about shooting at varying distances, but also something about judging distances -- and even about a deer's anatomy.

I enjoy shooting and looking at paper targets, but this soon bores me. I like to see things happen when I shoot. So a few years ago I started borrowing ideas from the local archery club's field course.

Always try to shoot from a solid rest, or at least from a solidly rested position, such as shooting from a sitting position.

At the time I was taking care of several ranches in the Texas Hill Country that had many natural backstops. With this in mind I cut out of plywood several full-body deer targets. These were then placed throughout one of the pastures at ranges from 100 yards to a little over 400 yards. On the day of the "shoot" I inflated balloons to approximately 12 inches in diameter to duplicate a deer's vitals. The balloons were taped to the life-size targets where the vitals would be. Later I walked the course, and shot at the balloons. I knew immediately if I would have cleanly taken the deer. While this was a little more trouble than simply shooting at paper, it was much more interesting! I have used the technique several times when teaching practical deer hunting seminars.

OPTICS

Scopes, binoculars and spotting scopes are mandatory everyday equipment for the hunter interested in taking mature white-tailed bucks. In other words, optics are extremely important.

I already have discussed how to use variable scopes as range estimators and this certainly is a good reason to use them. A primary purpose of a scope is to magnify the target, making that target easier to see. But a scope serves other purposes as well.

A scope also places the target on one plane, essentially the same as the reticle. (With iron sights your eye constantly is trying to focus on the target, rear sight and front sight. As you get older your eyes change, making it increasingly difficult to shoot accurately with open sights.) A scope enhances vision under poor light conditions. However, the best reason for using a scope is precise shot placement at distances near and far.

Good optics are paramount when hunting mature whitetails.

Scopes, as mentioned, allow a considerably better view of a target under poor light conditions. Many of today's scopes use lenses coated with special light-gathering chemical formulas. These make it much easier to see a target extremely early in the morning or late in the afternoon when some mature bucks are apt to move. This visual advantage also makes identifying a target much easier, and thereby makes hunting much safer. That alone should make scopes an important consideration.

The trend toward large front optics

The early 1990s witnessed several new trends in rifle scopes. Many "modern" hunters are using scopes with large front optics (50mm and larger), with coated lenses provide great light gathering abilities for hunting under poor light conditions, just as mentioned. Some of these scopes make it possible to see well before and past legal shooting hours. But they also are of great benefit on overcast days when the light is "flat."

Although such scopes offer definite advantages, they also have some disadvantages, which include added weight and the need for extremely high mounts and rings. This puts the center of the scope and the required line of sight high above the comb of the rifle. Shooting accurately with this arrangement, therefore, takes some practice. Some of these scopes are so large they remind me of someone mounting a stove pipe on their rifle. But, I cannot criticize too loudly, because several of my rifles wear variable scopes with up to 50mm front objective optics.

Choosing the right finish

The finishes of scopes are many, varying from the high lustre blue, to matte and crinkle finishes, to silvery stainless steel. The introduction of over-the-counter silver-colored stainless steel rifles has created interest in the stainless scopes to match the rifles. While these combinations are attractive in a modern sort of way, the bright silver barrels and actions and silver scopes are highly visible even at great distances. Their finishes may reflect light minimally, but they are still light in color. This is something that serious deer hunters should consider.

Please do not get me wrong. I truly like the stainless steel rifles, having owned -- and I still own -- several. They are highly accurate and durable. Thankfully most of the metal parts of my stainless rifles have a matte or Parkerized finish that distorts light rather than reflecting it. This helps considerably. In addition, several of my stainless rifles have been blued.

With the interest in camouflage, and the introduction of rifles completely finished in the popular camouflage patterns such as Realtree and Mossy Oak, several scope manufacturers now offer scopes finished in the same camo patterns. These blend in with most backgrounds and allow the user some movement without detection.

Many rifles and scopes reflect brightly when the sun shines on their highly polished finish. This warns any deer in the woods that a hunter is present, or at least that potential danger is in the immediate area. This is an excellent reason not to use glossy finished stocks, as well as highly polished and blued rifles and scopes. While a young buck might pay little attention to the reflection, a mature buck certainly will.

Using a binocular

A binocular should be a hunter's constant companion, especially a hunter seeking mature deer. What better way to spot and evaluate a buck than through a binocular? My preference for a binocular is a 10X by 42. While others might prefer something less powerful, I like the 10-power's greater magnification. With such power I not only can spot and evaluate game at long distances, I also can pick out the slightest movement when hunting in dense cover, or determine how many points a buck has, even if he is partially obscured by underbrush.

Many hunters seem to think binoculars are important only when hunting in wide open country. But as I've just stated, there are many advantages to using a good binocular even when hunting in dense cover or if you are a woods hunter. However, when hunting in the open country of the Southwest and West they are extremely important. A binocular not only can help me to spot and evaluate a buck, but also to plan a stalk.

One of the best hunters I have ever seen at this game of spotting whitetails and then stalking them is wildlife biologist/outfit-

Today's rifle comes complete with totally camouflaged stocks and actions, as well as scopes.

Stainless steel rifles, even though they are a bit brighter, are ideal for hunting in adverse weather conditions. From top to bottom, Remington's Model 700, Browning's A-Bolt Stalker, Ruger's Model 77 All Weather, Modern Muzzle Loading's MK-85, and Thompson/ Center's Contender Carbine.

ter/guide Greg Simons, who owns Wildlife Systems based in San Angelo, Texas. Greg is a master of locating whitetails at a distance with both binocular and spotting scope. He attributes his success at finding deer with hunting optics to knowing what to look for, where to look and when to look. Greg normally starts early in the morning by setting up on a ridge where he can see other ridges and valleys. In the morning the whitetails in his area return from feeding areas and bed down for the morning and possibly the rest of the day.

On a recent whitetail hunt with Greg in northwestern Texas we set up on the top of a ridge, arriving there well before first light. When daylight arrived, while Greg peered through his 20X Leupold spotting scope, I scanned the opposite slope with my binocular.

"Got one," Greg whispered. "He's just below that biggest tree in the bottom of the draw." Greg pointed, and I followed the line from his outstretched finger. After several moments I finally located the bedded buck, well over a half-mile away. He was a good mature deer for the area, long tines with decent mass and spread.

"He's one we ought to take a closer look at," Greg advised. "See the lay of the land down below? We should be able to drop off the backside of this ridge and use that thick line of brush down to the right of the buck to get closer, then move over to the ravine right behind where the buck is bedded. With any luck we should be able to pop up about 50 yards from the buck - provided the wind doesn't switch

Outfitter/guide Bill Whitfield prepares to scan the distant brushline using a Swarvoski binocular.

around or go to swirling on us. I suspect the buck will stay bedded right there for the next couple of hours, if he behaves like they normally do."

Shortly thereafter we moved down the backside of the ridge. About an hour later we had completed the perfectly executed stalk, thanks to Greg's knowledge of the deer, the area we were hunting, and his abilities with hunting optics, not only to spot and evaluate the buck but also to plan the stalk.

The following year Greg and I pulled off a similar stalk on a whitetail in the mountainous country of far West Texas. We spotted the

Guide/outfitter Greg Simons is a master at using optics to spot and then planning a stalk, to take big mature whitetails.

buck from well over a mile away, then planned our stalk according to a plan developed by "reading" the land with our hunting optics. The final portion of that stalk was truly interesting as we were interrupted several times by deer. When we finally neared the buck, he seemed to disappear, and practically did in some tall grass. Only by using binoculars, even at the close range of less than 50 yards, could we have spotted just the tip of his antlers protruding above the tops of the grass.

Regardless of whether you hunt out West or in the dense forests of the East, learn how to use and get the most out of your hunting optics. Doing so certainly will increase your odds, not only of seeing deer and quickly evaluating their antler development and age, but also of making a quick and true shot.

CHOICES OF THE EXPERTS

Among hunters there are many who justifiably have earned the right to be considered *expert* deer hunters. Over the years it has been my pleasure to have hunted with many whom I consider to be among the best deer hunters in the late twentieth century. With your indulgence, I have selected several hunters from various parts of the country whom I consider to be among the best of deer hunters.

In most instances these people not only are excellent deer hunters who have hunted whitetails throughout North America, they also are fellow writers, and in some instances wildlife biologists as well. Their whitetail experiences are varied and vast. They hunt primarily with rifles, but most also have hunted and taken mature whitetails with muzzle loaders, shotguns, handguns, and bow and arrows as well. I hope you will find their choices of firearms and optics interesting and helpful.

J. Wayne Fears

Wayne is a wildlife biologist, former outfitter/guide, dedicated white-tailed deer hunter, and one of the most respected and widely read outdoor writers in the business. The author of numerous books, his *Hunting Whitetails Successfully* is the highest selling white-tailed deer hunting book on record.

He has hunted whitetails throughout most of their range in North America. His favorite buck was a near record-book eight point he took in Randolph County, Alabama.

Fears' preferred whitetail rifle is a Ruger Number 1 International, custom chambered for the .280 Remington. The single shot is topped with a fixed power Leupold 6X scope. I occasionally have conned this hunting partner into letting me use it when we've hunted together. Wayne's choice of ammunition for the .280 Rem when hunting whitetails is the 160 grain Winchester Supreme.

J. Wayne Fears, one of my hunting partners, knows the value of spending time on the range and in the field shooting under hunting conditions.

Bill Bynum

Bynum, a native of western Tennessee, in many ways is like the legendary Davy Crockett -- both grew up in the same region. Bill is one of the finest woodsmen with whom I have ever shared a hunting camp. A serious deer hunter with considerable experience, a respected writer, and a frequent seminar speaker who addresses whitetail hunting, Bill is considered an expert on deer scents.

Bill's favorite whitetail rifle is a Ruger Model 77, Mark II All-Weather stainless, chambered for the .300 Winchester Magnum. His choice in scopes is a 3.5 to 10X Simmons Whitetail Classic. The rifle's best shooting ammunition is PMC's Eldorado 165 grain X-bullet.

Gary Machen

Gary Machen is a Texas rancher, who, in my opinion, is one of the best whitetail hunters I ever have accompanied. He is knowledgeable in the ways of hunting whitetails and also in producing them on his ranches -- management programs on his properties have produced several Boone & Crockett record book contenders. Gary has hunted throughout North America for whitetails and has taken several monstrous whitetails. His largest trophy is a typical buck that exceeds Boone & Crockett minimums, taken in Canada moments after I missed the buck.

Gary's favorite whitetail rifle is a custom Winchester Model 70 chambered for the .270 Winchester, built by Texan Bill Wiseman. His choice in scopes is a Zeiss 2.5 by 10X with a 52mm front objective lens. His favorite load for whitetails is comprised of 140 grain Nosler Ballistic Tip bullets pushed by 58.5 grains of IMR 4831 powder.

Charles Alsheimer

Charles Alsheimer, from New York, is one of our country's most gifted wildlife hunter/photographers. His action-packed photos portray a special intensity. Charles also is a respected outdoor writer who specializes in white-tailed deer.

Charlie's favorite rifle is a Remington Model 700 chambered for the .270 Winchester, which has been customized by the addition of a synthetic Bell & Carlson stock. The rifle is scoped with a Leupold 2.5 by 8X Vari-X III. His favorite whitetail load uses 130 grain Nosler Ballistic Tip bullets propelled by 55 grains of Dupont 4350 powder.

Alsheimer also hunts frequently with a shotgun. His favorite is a 12 gauge Remington Model 11-87 using a 22-inch Hasting slug barrel. The shotgun is scoped with a Leupold 1.5 to 5X. The slugs he most often uses are Winchester's 3-inch Hi-Impact Sabot Slugs.

Jay Gates

Jay Gates has hunted deer throughout North America, but seems to specialize in whitetails and Coues whitetails. He has taken several record book Coues whitetails, and several near-record whitetails. Jay has written numerous articles, as well as a book about his deer hunting experiences.

Gates, a native of Arizona, is without a doubt one of the country's most knowledgeable deer hunters. His favorite rifle is a Remington Model 700 customized by Ed Higgins of California. It is chambered for the .270 Winchester and topped with a fixed 6X Zeiss scope. His favorite loads include 130 grain Hornady Custom factory ammunition, and handloads which use 130 grain Flat Base Sierra bullets in front of 58 grains of H4831 powder.

Jay Gates is one of the best deer hunters in North America, especially when it comes to hunting mature whitetails. Here he shows off huge buck taken in Texas.

Richard P. Smith

Richard P. Smith has considerable and wide experience as a deer hunter, and is also an accomplished and highly respected writer. He has written numerous deer hunting related books. His best buck is a monstrous drop-tine buck taken in Saskatchewan, Canada.

This Michigan resident's favorite rifle is a Remington Model 700 chambered for the .30-06. Richard's old .30-06 has held numerous scopes of several makes and models during the years. His favorite whitetail ammunition is Remington's 150 grain Pointed Soft Point factory ammo.

*Richard P. Smith, a field editor for **Deer & Deer Hunting** magazine has taken some extremely fine mature whitetails with his favorite rifle.*

Richard also hunts with a .50 caliber Modern Muzzle Loader Knight MK-87 rifle. His favorite load for the muzzle loader uses a sabot with a .44 jacketed hollow point bullet, propelled by 100 grains of Pyrodex.

David Morris

David Morris is a wildlife biologist, guide, photographer, writer, book author (*Hunting Trophy Whitetails*, fast becoming a classic) and dedicated whitetail hunter who has hunted whitetail throughout North America, from Canada into Mexico. Several of David's bucks have barely missed recognition in the Boone & Crockett record book. His favorite buck, up to the time of our visit was an old 10 point with a gross score of 178 Boone & Crockett points.

Morris' favorite whitetail rifle, a customized Remington Model 700 built for him by Dale Hutcherson of Pasadena, Texas, uses a stainless, fluted barrel and a Lee Six fiberglass stock. It is chambered for the 7mm Remington Magnum and is topped with a Swarovski 3 by 9X scope. The load he has developed for whitetails for this particular rifle uses 140 grain Nosler Partition bullets propelled by 71.5 grains of Hercules Reloader 22 powder.

A Personal Choice

The author with a decent, mature whitetail taken while hunting with a single-shot Thompson/Center TCR'87 rifle.

I now would like to briefly describe my two favorite hunting firearms. My favorite rifle is a customized Remington Model 700 featuring an octagonal stainless steel barrel, a Timney trigger, stainless steel receiver, Winchester style bolt release, and a "Black T" teflon metal finish. The stock is an MPI Kevlar model. This rifle was built for me by MacGillivray Rifles of Paso Robles, California. The rifle is topped with a Simmons Whitetail Classic 3 to 10X scope. My favorite whitetail load for the rifle uses 140 grain Nosler Ballistic Tip bullets.

Previously I have stated my favorite handgun is a customized Thompson/Center Contender with an SSK Industries .309 JDJ

The author shooting one of his favorite handguns, a .309 JDJ Contender.

ported 14-inch barrel. The handgun is topped with a Simmons 2.5 by 7X handgun scope. My favorite whitetail ammunition for the handgun uses 150 grain Nosler Ballistic Tips.

But no matter what members this group of expert hunters have chosen as their favorite whitetail guns, you need to find your favorite -- what works best for you. And regardless of your choice of deer hunting gun and optics, learn everything you can about them, and spend considerable time practicing with them, not only at the range but also under field conditions. It will pay off in the future.

Chapter 9

Early Season Bucks

At first only one buck stood at the edge of the field. His velvet covered antlers, backlit by the late August afternoon sun, created an illusion of a huge, multi-faceted halo. He was watching two does feeding in the middle of the green field.

Moments later three other bucks appeared at the edge of the field. After assuring themselves no danger lay in or around the field they boldly strode in and started feeding on the lush forage. By the time darkness had obscured my vision several more bucks of varying sizes had appeared in the field. I watched them intently, alternating between my binocular and spotting scope.

Though I carried a camera with a telephoto lens the distance was too far for good photos. But I did take time to sketch drawings of the bucks' basic antler styles and configurations in the buck journal I maintain for such purposes. Thus, if I saw them again, I would know it. Under the cover of darkness I stole away. The deer never knew I was anywhere in their territory, but that was by design.

Bucks in late summer

During the late summer, bucks are anxiously eating all they can to put on weight that will carry them through the lean times of the breeding season and fall. Because of their developing antlers they tend to live in relatively open bottomlands, near fields, areas where there is plenty to eat and where their growing antlers will not be scratched or injured. That is, if the habitat will allow.

It is not uncommon for white-tailed bucks to form bachelor herds, comprised essentially of bucks in the same age class, during the summer as they bucks are developing antlers. These bachelor herds vary in size from two to about 30.

The largest group of bachelor bucks I have observed numbered 27. All the bucks in the herd appeared to be at least three years old or older, each displaying eight or more points. I saw the group often that summer. Sometimes 27 bucks were in the group, sometimes fewer, but basically it was the same group, easily recognized by their developing antlers. The bucks traveled together as a loosely knit group. At times they groomed each other, at other times they appeared to be at odds with each other, not unlike one large and happy family. I kept tabs on this group from the late part of July until they disbanded the first week of November. During their last couple of weeks together they became increasingly intolerant of each other, frequently sparring and eventually fighting with one another seriously.

Late summer bucks for the most part stay in their same pattern during the early fall.

Some research suggests that bachelor groups form so bucks can establish their positions within the area, before such questions are settled by all-out fights. These bachelor bucks also tend to disperse before the beginning of the rut, before all the serious fighting starts as the peak of the rut begins. The peak of the rut in the part of the country where the aforementioned bucks lived usually did not begin until the second week of December.

I could find those bucks nearly any afternoon during the late summer and early fall. They tended to roam in the same basic area every day. But when the gun season started during the second week of November, many of the bucks already were drifting into areas where they would spend the fall. By the third week of November they had altered completely their late summer patterns.

Such was the case of the four bucks mentioned at the beginning of this chapter. They each were four years old or older and carried magnificent antlers. I had watched them grow up and grow smart in the ways of humans. Until the hunters arrived to hunt during the rut, the bucks were seen quite regularly, at least during October, which coincided with archery season in that area. Until the beginning stages of the rut were seriously underway, the bucks remained in their late summer patterns. But when the bucks dispersed, all bets were off as to where they could be found.

Some bucks, even mature bucks with impressive antlers such as those mentioned, tend to be creatures of habit, at least during the late summer. They bed, feed, water, and travel predictably. Unless greatly disturbed they will follow the same basic routines day after day, until the onset of rutting activities.

I find it humorous to hear hunters talk about patterning mature bucks. My opinion, based on many years of hunting and research, is that patterning bucks during the fall -- once the breeding season begins -- is an impossibility. In fact, during this time mature bucks tend to pattern hunters more than the other way around.

Patterning a buck for opening day

There is, however, an exception to the "rules of patterning." In the late summer it is fairly easy to pattern some bucks, as long as you do not get too close or too familiar with them. However, with the onset of the breeding season all those late summer patterns are altered.

Research has shown some bucks may even leave the area where they spent the summer and early fall. Several bucks I have watched throughout the summer were no longer to be found when the regular gun season opened. In some instances, if the bucks were in some way distinguishable, I have seen them several miles away only a couple of weeks later.

As mentioned, during the summer deer are somewhat more tolerant of humans than they are in the fall as hunting seasons approach. Take advantage of this, as well as the fact that they continue their late summer routine into the archery season -- and sometimes into the first few days of the gun season, and one of those big bucks you watched all summer might be yours for the taking.

One of my best bucks, a deer with 14 total points and legitimate 6-inch bases, was taken on opening day. This in an area where most hunters do not start hunting until much later in the season as the rut approaches.

I initially had located the buck during a summer scouting trip to the ranch. The farmer who leased the tillable land on the property had mentioned seeing a buck in May that looked as if a couple of fence posts were growing from his head. By the time I could spend a few days on the ranch, it was mid-July when temperatures can surpass the century mark. Water in that thirsty land is at a premium. The only sources for drinking water, therefore, are several ponds near windmills, scattered throughout the rather flat terrain. The farmer suspected the buck lived at the extreme southern part of the property.

Late in the afternoon I positioned myself in a windmill tower, from which I had a commanding view of the area around me. The waterhole was about a hundred yards away. As the afternoon progressed I watched a procession of javelina, feral hogs, quail, coyotes, bobcats, numerous does, as well as some bucks come to water.

One of the bucks showed considerable promise, if you like wide bucks. Although not yet completely developed, the buck, which I guessed as a two-year-old had a 10 point rack showing with about a 24-inch outside spread. Given the opportunity to mature, I suspected he would bear further attention in a couple of years.

Just at dark I spotted "my" buck standing at the edge of the brush. He stood still for a long time, then walked to the water's edge, splashed in up to his knees and drank deeply. His thirst sated, he turned and disappeared into the dense brush.

Not until the middle of September did I return to the ranch to check the progress of "my" 6-inch buck. The occasion was a hunt for mourning doves, with which the area abounded. My role in the hunt was to host several business associates and guests of the ranch owner.

Loading up the hunters along with several containers of iced-down soft drinks, I dropped them off at various waterholes, telling them I would return at dark to pick up them and their birds. That task finished, I headed to the pond where in July I had seen the 6-inch buck. I set up a tripod where I could see not only the waterhole but also several open lanes through which deer might approach the area.

No sooner had I crawled into the tripod, than animals started appearing, as well as hundreds of mourning doves. In spite of nearly being covered up with doves, I never loaded my shotgun. I was much more interested in seeing the massively antlered buck than shooting doves. I did not have to wait long.

The buck appeared in one of the lanes leading to the waterhole. His antlers, still covered with velvet, were truly impressive. Their spread appeared to be over 17 inches on the outside of the beams, but that mattered little because of the overall mass. I wished it were deer season and that my over-under shotgun were a rifle or handgun.

The buck spent little time drinking. As soon as he had finished, he disappeared into the dense underbrush on the other side of the pond. Several other bucks came to water there that afternoon but none were nearly as impressive as the massively antlered buck.

I scheduled myself to be on the ranch the afternoon before the mid-November opening of the hunting season. The temperature that day was warm, with a stout breeze blowing from the southwest. The weather likely would be similar in the morning, perhaps a little cooler, but not much.

Based on my two summer sightings of buck, I surmised he visited the waterhole in the evening. Would he be there in the morning, or even in the area in the morning? I was not certain.

That night I worked on ranch reports dealing with hunting season recommendations, then later on a magazine article that soon would be due. What little remained of the night passed quickly.

Well before daylight I was sitting in an area not far from the pond, near a recently harvested milo field. Quite a few stalks remained standing in the field and along its edges -- part of our management plan to insure the wildlife would have sufficient food during the winter. With the coming of first light I spotted a couple of does and fawns, then watched a young forkhorn work a scrape, which apparently only recently had been opened.

Scanning the horizon I spotted the top of a bush shaking vigorously. There was no wind, but the bush kept shaking. Without a doubt a buck was rubbing on the bush. Try as I may I could not see through the brush to the source of the movement. All I could do was wait. Had the rut been closer I likely would have tried rattling horns to entice the buck out of the cover, but my rattling horns were miles away. I waited.

What seemed an eternity actually took only about 10 minutes. Finally the bush stopped its shaking. I wondered whether the buck would come my way or go another. I also wondered if indeed the buck making a rub would be the massively antlered buck I was seeking. Still I waited. There was little else I could do.

Then, at the edge of the opening not far from where the bush shook, stepped a buck. I dropped my binocular to my chest, raised the Remington rifle and gazed through the variable scope turned up to five power. I clearly could see the buck had massive main beams with what looked like a lot of antler material on his head. It was "my" buck! When the cross-hairs momentarily settled on the buck's shoulder I squeezed the trigger.

In moments I approached the downed buck. There was little doubt he was the mature buck I had seen earlier in the summer. His rack was magnificent. He was a basic 10 point with double brow tines, two long basal "kickers" and extremely massive beams. Both sides measured better than 6 inches in circumference. He remains the most massively antlered buck I have taken in over 40 years of hunting whitetail.

I have seen only one other buck while hunting that appeared to be more massive. That buck showed up in a *sendero* (Spanish for a lane or path cleared through thick brush) in Mexico. Unfortunately, he was well over a thousand yards away as I looked him over through a 20X spotting scope, then watched him walk away never to be seen again. Hopefully, sometime there will be another one like him, only then may he be much closer!

The bow hunter's advantage

In recent years we have seen bow hunters consistently take some of the finest and largest whitetails harvested each year. I believe the reasons for this are several. One reason is that we have seen great advances in archery equipment. Today's bows are faster and more powerful than ever. Never have there been finer and straighter arrow shafts or sharper broadheads. And never have there been more bow hunters in modern times than there now.

Thanks to the interest in bow hunting and bow hunters' activism, there now are archery seasons that begin in the early fall and generally precede the gun or muzzleloader seasons. This gives bow hunters the chance to hunt deer before they become overly wary, or before they change from their late summer patterns.

The author comes to full draw while bowhunting. Archery seasons are ideal times to take big, mature bucks.

If they pattern bucks during the late summer, bow hunters have the opportunity to hunt those deer long before firearm hunters do. Not a bad combination or finer advantage! This is not an expression of sour grapes on my part, but merely a statement of facts. Bow hunters do have many advantages at their disposal, but it is up to them to determine how best to use those advantages.

In my experience bow hunters tend to be extremely skillful and attentive hunters. They have to be. They also learn how to read and interpret sign, blend in with their respective backgrounds, and be ever patient. If a bow hunter locates a mature buck through summer scouting and carefully hunts him during the first part of the hunting season, he can expect an excellent opportunity to loose an arrow at the buck.

Understanding food

In many ways the key to early season deer is food. As mentioned, during the early fall bucks are eating as much as possible to prepare for lean times. Does are trying to recover from rearing fawns and prepare for producing more. Weaned fawns are seeking food so they can survive on their own. For all deer the early fall is a "hungry" period.

Knowing what deer eat in the early fall during bow season or the first few days of rifle season can contribute greatly to hunting success. Such information is available from several sources, most notably the wildlife or natural resources department of the state in which you hunt. Most such departments are headquartered in the state capital, with field biologists and wardens located strategically throughout the state. Another

Knowing where to find the primary food source, lead the author to this Southeastern whitetail.

good sthat have established wildlife management curriculums. Most of these universities conduct considerable research in the wildlife field.

Both kinds of sources normally are happy to provide deer food habit information to those who ask. In some instances these two entities conduct field days that are open to the public, on state-owned wildlife management areas. These can prove invaluable, especially if you do not mind asking questions. Seminars presented at local outdoor sport or hunting shows also may provide such information. In any case, learn not only what deer eat at certain times of the year (in this case the early fall), but also learn to identify those plants or mast crops, and where to find them in the area you hunt.

115

If someone takes a deer before I do in the early part of the season, I try to gain a look at the deer's rumen so I can learn firsthand what the local deer are eating. It may not always be easy to identify the chewed portions of plants in a deer's rumen, but generally you will be able to ascertain the key items.

Should you learn what deer eat during the early season, note it in your buck journal, but also note in your journal or on your map *where* those plants exist relative to your hunting area. Also try to identify not only the primary food items, but also the secondary choices.

If you can locate squirrels in the late summer and early fall, there too you will find deer, primarily because of the mutually shared food supplies.

Knowing prime early season food items can spell success, such as knowing where in the Southeast there are persimmon trees with ripe fruit.

Throughout much of the South and Southeast, white oak acorns are the whitetails' favorite mast food items. But what if for some reason the white oaks do not "make" that particular area? What will deer turn to then? In some areas apples are favored food items, but if no apples appear that fall, what is the deer's next favorite food item? The same is true with persimmons in the Southeast. If there are none or only very few, what is their next favorite choice? Knowing will make a difference in being able to find deer in the early fall. Some food items are eaten later in the fall, others later in the winter, and some whenever they are available.

Bait and mature bucks

In some states a deer's food supply may be augmented by choice deer food items, which is a fancy way of saying baiting is legal in some states. I will not discuss the ethical aspects of baiting. To me, choosing whether or not to hunt a legally baited area is a personal decision. I have hunted successfully over bait, and in the area where I grew up it was both legal and accepted as ethical.

Acorns provide high carbohydrate diets as the deer prepare for the breeding season and the coming winter. Knowing where to find acorns and how to identify favorite oak masts, can bring success to the early season hunter.

I have seen only a few big mature deer attracted to bait, and then generally before or after the season. Few, if any, truly big mature bucks have ever been shot *over* bait, contrary to what some people would lead us to believe. However, I have shot several good mature bucks *near* bait. Bucks tend to "hang around" does during the fall breeding season, which often coincides with the fall hunting season, and does tend to frequent bait.

Such was the case with a big buck I shot several years ago on a huge south Texas ranch. The buck was shot about 200 yards from a bait station. From my tripod I could see does feeding on corn strewn along a pasture road. I also could see a big buck approaching the top of a ridge where he could see the does and the surrounding countryside. However, he never came close to the does at the bait site. But when the does headed in his direction the buck fell in behind them. At that point I squeezed the trigger.

The pre-rut

The early season is often referred to as the pre-rut, which starts at the time the bucks shed their velvet. In northern climes the velvet normally starts coming off during the first week of September. In southern Texas velvet shedding normally occurs the second week of September. In most instances the velvet comes off within a 24-hour period. During the next month bachelor herds of bucks that have been traveling together begin breaking up slowly.

As their velvet comes off, the bucks spend considerable time rubbing their antlers to strengthen their neck muscles. Through sparring and posturing they start establishing dominance, to determine

Summer scouting while the bucks are in velvet is an ideal time to learn about whitetail behavior.

their position within the herd. Bucks, especially mature bucks, start drifting to the areas they have chosen, based largely on security and seclusion. During the pre-rut bucks do not show much interest in does.

During this period, signs such as rubs and initial scrapes may be plentiful. Some of these scrapes may be boundary scrapes, some may be returned to in the future, and some may never again be visited. In my experience, regardless of what kind of scrapes these first attempts are, as soon as scrapes are activated the bucks can be rattled up, even during the pre-rut period. The techniques, however, are not the same as those normally used later in the rut.

Taking a mature deer during the early fall may not be an easy chore once the pre-rut period has begun. Nonetheless, never overlook the possibility of taking a mature buck early in the hunting season, before he changes from his late summer routine. It may well be the best time to take a particular buck.

Chapter 10

Hunting the Rut

It was mid-December in the south Texas brush country. A brisk northerly breeze had dropped the late fall temperatures to just above freezing. This was one of those deer hunting days people dream of experiencing.

During the early morning we had seen numerous bucks of all sizes. Some obviously were roaming, actively seeking does. Others were chasing does or making moves on them. Two days before, few deer seemed to be in the area, and now they appeared to be coming out of the woodwork! The moon of madness was upon the local deer population.

We had passed up several bucks, though one buck really had caught our attention. While watching a pair of young bucks chase a doe we happened to see the buck waiting in the brush. As the doe headed his way the buck suddenly stepped out of the brush and made a threatening move toward the two young bucks.

The buck was the kind most hunters come to South Texas to find. His rack was long-tined, wide and massive. But before we could react he picked up the doe's trail and suddenly both were gone. We hunted the area for a while hoping to again catch a glimpse of the deer, but were unsuccessful. After a while we decided to drive to a new area, promising to return later that afternoon and hunt the area where we had seen the big buck.

The narrow road we traveled led through a dense thicket. Not 20 steps ahead, a doe crossed our path, running as if something were after her. I noticed her tail was held horizontally, sticking straight out from her body. I often had seen does in estrus carrying their tail in a similar manner. As quickly as she was there, she disappeared into the dense brush on the other side of the *sendero*, or path.

I quickly instructed my companion to drive to the exact spot where the doe had crossed the road, then cut the engine. He did. Immediately after we had stopped the pickup a buck with a massive six point rack literally ran into the side of the truck. He hit with enough force to make quite a dent in the side of the old ranch truck and then fell. The buck lay on the ground for a few moments, then stood up, shook himself, walked around the front edge of the truck and again picked up the doe's trail!

We could hardly believe what had happened. As we stared at one another, almost in disbelief, another much larger buck ran out of the brush to cross the road. He stopped just long enough for us to get a good look at him, then disappeared as he trailed the doe. We never had a chance at him.

Back at camp we compared notes. Only one buck, a massively beamed, long-tined 10 point, was hanging from the meat pole. All the hunters in camp claimed to have seen numerous bucks, including some definite keepers. Each of us was anxious to learn where each hunter planned to spend his afternoon hunt -- and anxious to get back into the woods after a quick meal. Each of us had planned our hunt according to when we hoped the peak of the rut would occur. Historically in south Texas that was December 15. We were right.

Timing of the rut

The rut, in a way, is a misnomer. In the truest sense of the term, the rut spans the time bucks start shedding their velvet until the time the cast their antlers. But the term is used by most hunters to refer to the peak of the breeding season, when most of the does within the herd are coming into estrus.

Does and their hormones indicate when the peak of the breeding season occurs. Pinpointing the exact time when the rut will occur in any given area, therefore, is a bit difficult. Normally the dates vary little more than a few days from year to year. The primary controller of the breeding season is the amount of daylight hours. As the amount of sunlight decreases and reaches a certain level, the does' hormones start increasing, causing the ovaries to produce eggs. Bucks, on the other hand, are capable of breeding and are producing viable sperm from the time they shed their velvet.

The whitetails' fall breeding season and the timing of their antler development are affected significantly by photoperiodicity, the amount of daylight hours per day. Interestingly, in most areas the breeding season also ensures the birth of fawns during the time of the year's highest nutritional level. This is one of the reasons why in states such as Texas the earliest breeding season occurs in mid-August and the latest in late December.

In the south Texas brush country, noted for its big deer, the peak of the breeding season occurs generally between December 15 and 24. But, in central Texas, just above the brush country, the majority of breeding normally takes place in late October and early November. The same can be said of states such as Alabama, where the whitetail breeding season occurs during early November in certain parts of that state, yet not far away in the southern part of the state the rut occurs in late January. Surely the amount of daylight hours in various areas of the same state do not vary that greatly. Yet, there is a considerable difference between areas as to when spring "green-up" occurs.

Generally, however, it can be said the rut north of the 45th parallel begins about the 15th of November. In states such as New York the vast majority of the whitetail breeding occurs between November 10 and 30, with the 15th being the peak. In Wisconsin the whitetail may breed any time from the first of October until January 8, with the peak being November 10 through 29. By contrast, in Mississippi the peak reportedly occurs between December 18 and 31. These dates are based on research conducted in their respective states.

Variations in the breeding season from year to year can be caused by range or forage conditions; the body condition of both bucks and does; buck-to-doe ratios; the average age of does within the population; and even total deer densities. As mentioned, however, the timing of the rut in a given area normally varies little from year to year.

Jimmy Perlitz approaches a buck taken during the rut.

Nutrition and the breeding season

I am a firm believer that, to some extent, timing of the peak of the breeding season can be altered somewhat by greatly improving the nutritional conditions for the deer herd, and by making such nutrition available daily throughout the year. For several years I was involved in nutritional research at a high-fenced ranch in the Texas hill country. There we fed a free-choice pelleted ration, available 365 days of the year. The deer on the high protein, high energy, well balanced (mineral and vitamin) ration tended to breed two weeks later than those on a native seasonal diet right across the high fence. Coincidence? Perhaps. But it does make for some interesting speculation and discussion.

Research has shown that generally the mature does come into estrus first each fall. On the other hand, I have seen individual does which lost their fawns to predation, and which were in excellent fall body condition, come into estrus at least a month before the majority of the does in the local population. I also have seen young does, those born during the previous spring or summer, have their first estrus cycle in late January or February (in Texas).

The author shot this mature buck during the latter part of the rut, in an area where deer normally do not get to be huge.

On ranches I have managed, where the deer enjoyed an excellent year-round nutritional level, approximately 75 percent of the young does bred. Other areas have reported rates of incidence as high as 66 percent of the first year does being bred. In both instances they were bred fairly late, normally at least a month to six week after the peak of the rut.

White-tailed does can cycle once every 28 days as many as seven times each breeding season. However in most instances they tend to be bred, or "settled," in the first or second heat period.

The secondary rut

We Americans are great "splitters" and tend to split the whitetail's breeding season into primary and secondary ruts. For the most part the secondary rut is believed to occur about 28 days after the primary rut. The does that participate in the secondary rut are those that, for some reason, were not bred during the peak of the rut or did not conceive.

I think that, in many instances, the majority of the does in the secondary rut are those just coming into heat due to body condition, or because they produced late fawns and are just now regaining body condition to ovulate, or because they are just reaching puberty (in the case of the 6 to 10 month old does).

Some hunters and biologists who man check stations seem to think a number of the bigger bucks are taken during the secondary rut. Maybe this is because competition is high for the does that remain unbred. From my observations, some of the biggest bucks seen chasing does were those going after young does in their first head period during January and early February (in southern Texas).

Behavior of does in estrus

Does generally indicate their approaching estrus by producing pheromones. Bucks pick up on this quite readily, as do other does. I have watched several groups of does in which one member of a group was approaching her heat period. The doe approaching estrus was shunned and avoided by the others in the group. Why? I am not sure. But I have seen it happen several times. I also have seen does approach doe decoys drenched with "doe in heat" scent. As soon as they smell the scent they move away from the decoy.

A doe coming into estrus acts nervous, she may urinate frequently and walk around with her tail held straight out -- or even at "half mast." Some does may actually seek out individual bucks to sire their offsprings. Others are not selective. Remember, does are just as individual as bucks, or -- once again -- as individual as you or I.

Some does, when estrus approaches, visit scrapes and there trickle urine into the pawed out area on the ground. They might even paw the ground themselves. As they leave they trickle urine on the ground. When the buck checks his scrape he may pick up the trail of the doe and pursue her. I have watched this occur on several occasions. In one instance I sat watching a particularly active scrape. Based on how the deer were acting, I had guessed the peak of the breeding season was just about to start. A doe appeared and walked boldly to the scrape. There she urinated in the scrape and trickled urine as she walked away.

Less than a minute later a buck appeared downwind of the scrape, the direction the doe had taken. The buck, a big mature eight point, walked to where the doe had urinated on the ground, smelled it, lip-curled (flehmening, pronounced "flaming") and picked up the trail. As soon as he disappeared, I fell in behind him and took up their trail. A short time later three more bucks were on the trail of the doe. Thankfully the country was relatively open and I could keep up with their movements. I spent the rest of the morning following the doe and her entourage. Before I finally lost them when they crossed into someone else's property there were five bucks following the doe.

Bucks chasing does

The buck's pursuit of the doe is interesting to watch. The moves I have seen some bucks put on does were reminiscent of extremely good cutting horses separating one steer from the herd and then keeping him from returning to it. I also have seen bucks chasing does for long periods of time, and huge processions of bucks chasing a single doe.

One year, while hunting on an intensively managed ranch owned by a close friend, I watched 13 bucks chasing a doe. The doe crossed a fairly narrow opening, and the first buck to follow was a mere youngster. Each buck that followed was bigger than the preceding buck. The last one in line was truly a monster.

On another hunt in eastern Wyoming I shot the sixth buck in line following a doe. Often it pays to wait and see all the bucks that may be following a doe, especially in areas where there are several mature bucks.

The number of bucks which might be on the trail of a doe depends greatly on the number of does currently in heat and the number of bucks in a given area. As with many factors in deer hunting during the rut, there are a lot of "depends" involved.

Generally a doe in heat is interested in bucks for a period of 36 to 40 hours, during 24 hours of which she will stand to breed. Some bucks will stay with a doe in estrus for the entire time that she is in heat or as long as she acts remotely interested in his advances. Other bucks will spend only a short time with a doe before going to look for another receptive female. I have seen both.

For several years I was involved in a deer genetics study involving penned deer. One of the bucks in our pens would stay with a single doe which was in heat, regardless of what else was going on, including another doe coming into estrus. Regardless how many does were in heat, he stayed with one doe until her time had passed. Thankfully not many of the does came in heat on the same day. But if two did start the same day, he would not breed the second one until her next heat period. This practice was reflected in the fawning dates in that particular pen.

In the next pen was a buck with 24 does. If two or more does came into heat on the same day, he would breed one, then go on to the next one, until all were bred. He spent very little time with an individual doe. Again, this was reflected in the fawning dates. In that particular pen it was not unusual to have several fawns born on the same day.

I have seen similar situations in the wild. In the wild, however, a buck generally will stay with a doe as long as she shows any signs of being in heat. During that time he seldom will be far away. If she beds down he also will bed down. But as mentioned there also are does that will breed with several bucks during their heat period.

While many hunters are afield during the breeding season, a surprisingly small percentage have actually seen a buck breed a doe. I have talked to grizzled veteran hunters who have taken some monstrous bucks, and have spent their hunting lives in some of the best deer country imaginable, yet even they have not seen the actual breeding. Admittedly, the breeding act in deer takes a very short time. I have, nonetheless, seen bucks breed does several times, both in penned situations and in "open country."

During the breeding season, bucks are moody, irritable, and anxious to do battle with little provocation. They constantly are on the lookout for does -- as well as for bucks approaching their backsides. Almost constantly they are on the move, even within their core areas.

Fighting bucks

The rut is a difficult time for bucks, be they youngsters or mature bucks. The period takes its toll on bucks, through lack of eating and through the stresses inherent in fighting and chasing does. Hardly any of the bucks fight fair. I have seen some bucks die from injuries received during fights. Some get so worn down during a fight they simply cannot recover. Occasionally bucks get their antlers locked together and both die.

Recently I was hunting on a well-managed ranch where the buck-to-doe ratio was one-to-one, and better than 40 percent of the buck herd was four years or older. The peak of the rut was only about a week away. Buck fights had become common, as evidenced by an abundance of broken tines, and scrapes and scars on the bucks' necks and shoulders.

I had just crawled into my tripod when I heard two bucks fighting about 200 yards away. As soon as it began I crawled down and headed toward the ruckus. Both animals were three or four years old, and equally matched. The two bucks had their heads together and were trying their best to outdo the other. As they pushed each other over shrubs, underbrush and dried limbs, the racket sounded much more like that of two bull elk fighting than that of two much smaller white-tailed bucks.

I sat watching from my ringside seat, trying to learn as much as I could about such fights and how to imitate them when rattling. As I watched, several other bucks came by to investigate the fight. Some of those came charging in, hair standing on end and eyes bugged, ready to fight also. Others approached cautiously, slipping in, watching momentarily and then leaving.

I was enthralled. After about three or four minutes, I noticed a mature buck charging out of the brush. He made a run at the closest fighting buck and hit him full force, driving his tines deeply into the buck's rib cage. The blow made a sickening, crunching sound. The mature buck withdrew his antlers, blood glistening on their tips. Immediately the fight broke up. The gored buck took a few steps and lay down. After several minutes he was dead.

Highly mobile tripods can put the hunter in position to take a good deer.

At another time during the peak of the rut, I watched a mature buck walk over to a yearling buck and, without any posturing or prior notice, start goring the youngster. A couple of days later I found the youngster dead. The massive amount of puncture holes in his carcass from the other buck's antlers gave the appearance of several loads of buckshot.

During my years as a biologist I have found several bucks dead as a result of rutting activities. For bucks the rut is a time of excitement, danger and procreation. However, in no way is this an easy time for bucks, young or old.

As bucks prepare for the rut

For us hunters the rut is a special, exciting time when we look forward with great anticipation to deer moving. We never know what will step out next. It could be a young buck, or the mature buck we have long dreamed of seeing in our sights. Given a choice, the peak of the rut is when most hunters want to be afield to hunt. But, as has been mentioned, the peak of the rut varies from area to area, and requires some homework to determine.

Generally the breeding season can be split into essentially three distinct periods, the pre-rut, the peak of the rut and the post-rut. Understanding each of these periods and knowing how to hunt them not only can be exciting, but quite rewarding as well.

Allow me to regress a bit and discuss the pre-rut period. The pre-rut starts shortly after the bucks start shedding their velvet. It also is an interesting period to hunt. Each day deer behavior is different. Bucks which previously had been buddies in bachelor herds no longer seem to care much about each other. And each day they get worse. As mentioned, the key to hunting this pre-rut is finding high energy food sources.

Several seasons ago I saw firsthand the changes in bucks during the period we call the pre-rut. It was the middle of November. That afternoon I sat on a food plot where I could see 12 bucks. They all came into the field from the same direction and fed close to one another. Occasionally they stopped feeding and groomed each other by licking one another's necks. This type of activity lasted for a couple of days.

A few days later the same bucks entered the field. This time, however, they seemed not to like each other as much as they had only days earlier. If one buck drew too close to another, he received a hard stare accompanied by ears laid back in a threatening manner. If one buck came too close to another's backside, there were more threats.

The following day the bucks did not come into the field as a group, but came singly. That day they began sparring with one another. Though not serious fights, these sparring matches lasted anywhere from 10 seconds to about a minute. The sparring bucks eventually would pull apart, stare about at other bucks, then continue sparring -- or separate and spar with other bucks. One afternoon six separate sparring matches were taking place at the same time.

By the end of the week the bucks were displaying even greater animosity. If one buck drew too close to another, a serious fight soon followed. Sometimes an argument was settled with hard stares and acceptance of one buck's dominance. But most often any question of dominance was settled by fighting until one buck turned and ran. All the bucks in the initial group were mature bucks. Occasionally other groups of bucks, mostly younger ones, appeared in the field. Apart from chance meetings, however, no two groups associated with each other.

By the end of the week the bucks had pretty well dispersed to other areas -- selected because of their food sources, proximity to water, and the presence does within the area.

While watching the bucks I also noticed a change in their attitudes toward does. A few weeks earlier mature does seemed to be the dominant animals around prime feeding areas. Bucks would give way whenever a doe stared at them. But once the velvet came off of their antlers the bucks became dominant, especially those bucks older than yearlings.

In the early part of the pre-rut the bucks showed virtually no interest in the does. As the fall progressed they started showing a little more interest, at least to the point of occasionally checking on them by smelling their recently deposited urine. This shift in interest from food to does occurred very quickly.

Rubs and scrapes during the pre-rut

During the pre-rut as evidenced above, bucks spend a fair amount of time sparring with each other, rubbing their antlers and starting to make scrapes. In the early part of the rut bucks may rub their antlers to remove whatever velvet remains on their newly cleaned antlers. As the pre-rut progresses the bucks start spending much time rubbing their antlers on shrubs, bushes and trees, not only to strengthen their neck muscles for serious fights, but also to leave their "sign." To some of the rubs they will return again and again. Other rubs may never again be visited. Regardless, rubs definitely indicate the presence of bucks in an area.

I tend to think the size of a rub is some indication as to the size of the deer that made it. However, some research indicates no correlation between the size of a rub and the size of a deer. My opinion, however, is based on numerous years of working in areas with an abundance of big-bodied, mature bucks. I also have learned rubs can play an important role in hunting.

I like to hunt where there are big rubs -- not just one, but several. While there is no promise the buck will return to them with any regularity, rubs do indicate that bucks exist in the area. Big is a relative term, especially when referring to rubs. In some of the areas where I hunt, the biggest tree is less than 6 inches in diameter. In that area a rub on such a tree is as big as they come. In other areas with much larger trees, I have seen bucks rubbing on trees with diameters of 8 to 10 inches.

While hunting on the Sanctuary in Michigan a few years ago, we found rubs made on trees 12 to 14 inches in diameter. The largest rub I ever have found was on a tree that measured 16 inches in diameter. That property was noted for big deer. The best deer taken off that property was a buck with 24 points altogether, just missing a net score sufficient for listing in the Boone & Crockett record book.

On the same property I watched a buck nearly that size rub on a tree that measured 14 inches in diameter. Unfortunately I spotted him "working" the tree about a week before the hunting season, during the area's pre-rut period. I dearly would have loved to have taken him, for he was one of the biggest bucks I saw that entire year. Once the hunting season started, the buck was not seen again -- ever!

During the pre-rut, and especially toward the end of the period, bucks make a great many scrapes. Mature bucks often make scrapes in the same areas where they had scrapes the year before, if not under the same overhanging limbs.

Hunting the pre-rut

Hunting bucks during the early part of the pre-rut is considerably easier than during its final days. During the early days bucks can be found around abundant food areas, or near high energy mast crops such as persimmons, acorns and similar fruits and mast. Toward the end the bucks are on the move. They are a completely different animal than a few days earlier.

When hunting during this time, I look for trails connecting food sources to bedding areas. I have observed that mature bucks tend to bed in areas of relatively thick grass and underbrush. Such areas often are close to water, be they streams, seeps or other standing water. I also look for a series of rubs along these trails. By paying attention to which side of trees the rubs have been made you can get a good idea as to which direction the buck normally travels. This figured out I will set up a tripod or tree stand and hunt it for three days.

If after three days I've had no results, I switch to another area. If I've done my homework through post-season and summer scouting I already will have such areas chosen. I thus can hunt them with no need to scout during the hunting season -- and thus avoid "polluting" or "tainting" the area with my scent. Such areas should be marked on my topographical maps and recorded in my buck journal.

Admittedly, the pre-rut period can be a tough time to take a big buck. Earlier he probably could have been ambushed in the areas where he had spent the summer, but by now his late summer patterns likely have been altered considerably. During part of the pre-rut, deer movement during the daylight hours may start to slow, or the mature bucks may start adapting to the movement of hunters -- especially if there is considerable hunting pressure in the area.

Deer drives in the pre-rut

In many areas of the country the majority of the hunting season falls during the pre-rut period. With that being the case, must make the most of what is available. Sitting near food sources, watching trails between bedding and feeding areas, and even sitting where one or more scrapes is visible can be productive. This also is a time when many hunters use deer drives, especially if the season is about to close and nothing else seems to have worked.

Deer drives can be great fun if properly and safely conducted. They also can be highly successful. A major drawback? The shooter usually has to decide quickly whether or not to shoot, and must be able to shoot a running deer.

If the season ends before the beginning days of the rut, it is best to delay a drive until the latter part of the season. This is because a deer drive tends to alter how deer do things for a few days. We were faced with just such a situation a few seasons ago in eastern Wyoming.

Other methods had produced some buck sightings, but not of the bucks we wanted. However, my outfitter/guide, Richard Edwards of Douglas, Wyoming, knew a portion of a certain creekbottom held some big bucks, so we organized to drive that area. I was positioned on a high bluff overlooking the bottom. Richard and several others started pushing from downstream about a quarter mile away. No sooner had they started than a couple of does and their fawn slipped out in front of them. I waited patiently -- well, patiently might be stretching things a bit.

Moments after the does passed, I heard Richard shout, 'Big buck!' Seconds later I heard a couple of shots, then stared up the creek from where they had come. Several more shots were followed by shouts about the big buck getting away. Finally, at nearly 700 yards, I spotted the buck running. He had passed through the line of drivers, unscathed, and was heading toward a bridge on the interstate highway that divided the open season area from the closed season area. The buck was a monster, with massive, palmated main beams -- the kind I wished for a better look at. I saw him all too briefly, with no chance to get him in my cross-hairs.

Several minutes later Richard told us how he first had walked passed the buck, then noticed a thick patch of willows and grass right next to the flowing creek. He turned around and walked back to it, then all but kicked the buck to get him moving. When the deer took off, he moved in a hurry.

That afternoon we made another drive on a different creek. It proved much more successful and I took an extremely nice mature 11 point buck as the drivers pushed him past me.

The end of the pre-rut

As the tail end of the pre-rut period approaches, bucks sometimes can be rattled up if a passive form of rattling is used. The best chances of horn rattling success occur during the last few days of the pre-rut and the early stages of the peak of the rut. Bucks at this time are anxious to fight and prove themselves. Thus they are attracted to the sound of rattling antlers.

About two weeks before the pre-rut phases into the peak of the rut, bucks spend much time making and visiting scrapes. The testosterone level in their bodies is making them restless. They are preoccupied by their sexual desires that increase with each passing day. Bucks take out their aggression on existing rubs, and vigorously rub or even destroy small shrubs with their antlers. These new rubs, which some call "breeding rubs," are easily distinguishable because of their obvious freshness and the intensity with which they were attacked.

As the peak of the rut approaches, bucks spend considerably more time fighting with one another. These are serious "I'm gonna kill you!" fights, and not mere sparring matches typical of the pre-rut period. Mature bucks roam more, crossing into areas where other bucks live, so the chances of serious fights are greatly increased. Even if a buck does not vigorously establish an exact territory, he will not take lightly another deer's "cutting in" on his action.

Does at this time continue to be found primarily in close proximity to food sources, and frequently are visited by bucks checking estrus status. A buck approaches a doe with his head held low to the ground in typical rutting buck fashion. If the doe urinates, as described earlier, the buck will excitedly sniff the discharge, raising his head high and curling his upper lip -- the gesture called "flehmening" -- as he checks her status.

The travels of the buck become less and less predictable as he wanders in search of receptive does. Often the mature buck will bed near a group of does so he can keep tabs on them. Then suddenly the first does start showing signs of estrus -- and interest in bucks, and the deer woods turn from tranquility to feverish movement.

Although some people try to relate the change in the deer attitudes and activities to the onset of cool weather, the primary factor is the reduction in daylight hours. When the photoperiod decreases to a certain level, does start ovulating and the peak of the breeding season commences.

Cool or cold weather really has nothing to do with the rut. It would occur even if the normally cool days and cold nights remained hot. There still would be a peak of the breeding season. Cool weather simply makes the deer feel better, just as the cool weather of autumn is exhilarating to humans. After a long spell of warm weather and minimal activity, the cooler weather seems to make animals move more, especially during daylight hours. By contrast, in some areas where temperatures remain relatively high in the daytime, much of the actual chasing and breeding occurs after dark while the air is cooler. But cool weather or not, the rut will occur when the does determine the time is right.

Hunters' paradise: the peak of the rut

Hunting as the rut peaks, especially where there is an abundance of mature bucks, is the experience of a lifetime. I vividly recall my first real opportunity to hunt under such ideal conditions. The greatest difficulty seemed to be deciding when to shoot, and which bucks to pass up. Back then every buck looked like a monster to me. Thankfully my companion had experienced the peak of the rut in years past and knew what kind of deer were possible - - if only I did not squeeze the trigger prematurely.

The swelled neck of the buck the author is holding indicates the rut was in full swing when this buck was taken.

The first bucks we saw were 8 and 10 point bucks with spreads that barely reached the tips of their ears. The next buck was a wide 10 point, but with relatively short tines. He was with a doe and refused to leave her. When we approached within a hundred yards he ran off, but then immediately returned and circled a bush. We moved closer and he ran off again, then he returned and again circled the same bush. Finally he horned something on the ground. At that point the doe stood up and started running with the buck in hot pursuit.

Fewer than 10 minutes later we found three bucks chasing a doe, but my host insisted all were too small -- although they looked quite impressive to me.

For the next hour we saw bucks everywhere we went. Little bucks, medium sized bucks, and one or two that truly were big bucks. Yet, according to my friend, we had not even begun hunting. He insisted we simply were driving around looking, and he was showing me deer.

Three weeks earlier I had driven the same pasture roads with my friend and we scarcely had seen any deer. Now it seemed as if someone had opened invisible gates and let the deer out to play for our benefit.

On the first day we would hunt an area with an abundance of does, watch them for a while and then move on. The second day we hunted out of tripods in areas where the ranch hands had reported seeing some extremely big deer. During the morning hunt I spotted 37 different bucks. All but five had eight or more points. Throughout the morning, bucks chased does, ran across the lanes cut through the thick brush, visited scrapes established along the edges of the lanes, and stopped momentarily in open areas to feed on fresh green forage. I pinched myself many times, just to be sure I was not dreaming!

As we ate a quick tailgate lunch, we watched several bucks tending does in a big field. The meal finished, we moved toward the edge of a wide open grassy field with knee-high grass and a scattering of shrubs, seemingly a favorite area for bucks chasing does. The bucks apparently pushed does into these areas in order to keep an eye on them -- and on any possible competition that might approach.

At a little past high noon we pulled up to the field. Through my binocular I could detect a form in the grass about 300 yards away. I felt sure it was a deer, but the head was obscured behind a small shrub. As I intently watched the spot, a long-tined buck stood up just beyond the deer I was scrutinizing. He looked my way, apparently recognized us as potential danger and started running away. Suddenly he stopped, ran back to the spot from where he had come and lay down next to what I now suspected was a doe -- though I could not yet be certain. By then I had replaced the binocular with my rifle. The buck was better than any of the deer we had seen, and the more I pondered it, the more enamored I became with his tall 10 point rack.

I glanced at my companion. He also was showing interest in the buck. I asked him if the deer was shootable. He nodded. I easily could make out the top part of the buck's shoulder. Using a solid rest and an appropriate hold, when all seemed right I squeezed the trigger. The tell-tale sound of a solid hit drifted back to us as the shot echoed into the distance.

I felt a little sad about shooting the buck, as I normally do after having taken the life of an animal. Yet the buck had declined the opportunity to escape, and had returned to the doe.

I also felt extremely happy. I had taken an extremely fine 10 point buck. No doubt within the hour the doe would find herself another boyfriend.

How vigorous is the rut?

The beginning of the peak of the rut is, as mentioned, characterized by an increase in scraping and vigorous rubbing activity. When these signs become more evident the peak of the rut soon will follow. In my part of the country I also can discern the stage of the rut by the number of phone calls from fellow hunters, all asking, 'Are they running yet?'

The intensity of the rut depends, to a great extent, on the overall deer population density and the buck-to-doe ratio. If the ratio is narrow, say one-to-three or less, there is considerable competition for does. In other areas with many does per buck, there is less competition between bucks. Under those circumstances the rut might not be as vigorous.

I often am humored by people who claim that while the old bucks are doing all the fighting, the young bucks are doing the breeding. In most instances, if only young bucks are doing the breeding it is because there are few older aged bucks. Generally the young bucks do a great deal of "pestering" of the does, chasing them when they start coming into heat.

I have seen, as described earlier, numerous bucks chasing the same doe. The first in line tend to be young bucks. Further back the mature bucks follow. The merry chase may lead the bucks quite a way, and the young bucks will persist almost to the end. Then, when the doe is ready to accept a buck, the mature buck most likely will step forward and do the actual breeding. I have seen this happen many times.

The peak of the rut in some areas lasts no longer than a week, while in other areas it might last two weeks. (Remember, we are talking about the peak of the rut and not the length of the overall breeding season.) The first week of the peak normally is the most interesting. As the number of receptive does within the herd declines, so does the fervor of the bucks. By the end of the two week peak, bucks have become stressed and fatigued from constantly running does, as well as from fighting and being on the move. As the number of unbred does dwindles, I suspect some of the bucks may be almost glad, if indeed they have such emotions.

Slip-hunting during the peak

During the peak of the chasing, I hunt bucks in several ways, but mostly I hunt concentrations of does. If I find does, bucks will not be far away. This requires hunting around food sources and/or still-hunting. Still-hunting really is a misnomer because it means slipping along slowly in areas with considerable buck sign -- tracks, rubs and scrapes. I thus prefer to call it slip-hunting.

I especially like to slip-hunt in areas with relatively decent visibility. This allows me to stop periodically and glass the surrounding countryside for deer. If I see a buck chasing a doe I can follow the action. Fortunately, I often hunt on large properties with several hundreds of acres all to myself, so I don't have to worry about bumping into other hunters. Slip-hunting without other hunters, of course, is much safer. Slip-hunting also allows me to cover much more country than if I were sitting in one area and waiting. I have taken numerous mature deer while slip-hunting during the peak of the rut.

One of my favorite bucks, a typical 13 point, was taken while hunting in this manner during the peak of the rut. A cold north-easterly wind was blowing a fine mist, making the ground damp and quiet. I started the morning by watching a small food plot. At daybreak several six month old fawns grazed in the field. They were alone, another sure sign the rut was in full swing. During this time such youngsters are in total confusion. Does no longer want them close as estrus approaches. Bucks find them annoying, especially the young "nubbin" bucks. And because the young doe fawns have not yet reached puberty, they are of no interest to bucks. At least not for the present.

When nothing else showed, I started moving into the wind, stopping every few steps to glass the brush and open grassy areas before me. I heard a commotion coming my way, then spotted movement through the screening of brush up ahead. At first I thought I'd spooked a deer and it was leaving. Then I noticed a number of deer were coming directly toward me.

Hurriedly, I knelt behind a small tree and cranked the variable Simmons scope down to 3.5X and watched the deer. If they kept approaching they might cross a narrow opening about 40 yards away. The first deer through was a doe, followed by a young 10 point buck. Right behind him was a multi-pointed buck. I saw him only for an instant, but during that one heartbeat I could see he was at least a typical 12 point. My adrenaline level leaped.

To the right of where the buck momentarily had appeared was another opening. This time when the multi-pointed buck stepped out and offered a shot, I was ready. Had I remained sitting on the field I never would have had a chance at the buck.

A couple of years later, while hunting during the peak of the rut in western Kentucky, I had the opportunity to hunt an area leased by David Hale and Harold Knight of Knight and Hale Game Calls. Several drives had produced does and young bucks, but nothing that captured our interest. As the afternoon progressed, David and I headed to a relatively open hardwood bottom, where previously he had seen several good mature bucks. We stopped his vehicle on the downwind side of the bottom and proceeded to slip-hunt into the wind. The afternoon was dark, gray and cold. A storm was brewing to the north and threatened to drop either rain or snow.

No sooner had we moved about a hundred yards into the bottom than David spotted movement ahead. He pointed toward a doe. Right behind her stood a buck. They had not yet seen us. Hurriedly I moved to a large fallen limb, got a steady rest, and as the doe moved to one side fired a shot from one of my favorite .280 Remington rifles. The buck was a beauty, 10 points with about a 20-inch spread. Again, slip-hunting during the rut had paid a handsome dividend.

Driving the rut

Deer drives during the rut can work extremely well, especially in the northern climates where snow already is on the ground. Visible tracks make deer movement obvious, and sometimes reveal whether the passing deer was a buck or doe. In deeper snow the darkly stained hocks may touch the snow, leaving a small brown stain on the white snow.

I have had the opportunity to take part in several deer drives during the peak of the breeding season. Generally we have conducted the drives during the midday, rather than early in the morning or late in the afternoon. Such drives work best in areas where there is limited cover, such as areas where there has been an abundance of agricultural crops and little standing brush, or creekbottoms in relatively open prairie country. Each year many mature bucks are taken while hunters conduct deer drives.

Horn rattling works equally well during this period of the peak of the rut. Effective techniques for rattling various stages of the rut will be discussed in the next chapter.

Changes during the post-rut

In time the intensity of the rut decreases, although it may again flair about a month past the peak as more does come into heat, and again even later when some of the year's young does have their first heat period (labeled by some as the secondary and tertiary ruts). As the rutting activities slow, bucks start losing interest in does and again become more interested in eating and survival than in sex.

These last forays of interest in sex might well be the best time to take the biggest, mature bucks. For whatever reason this final hurrah seems to be when some of the best bucks of the year appear and abandon some of their wariness. In many states, unfortunately, the deer season already is closed when this occurs.

Sometimes, after the last of the does are bred, all the bucks seem to be gone. For a few days it appears as if they are lying low and not moving at all. Indeed, whenever the post-rut enters this stage, hunting becomes difficult. I know of no techniques that consistently produce bucks during this time. The only technique which has worked for me during this time of inactivity is slip-hunting areas of dense cover to root out the bucks.

During the peak of the rut, particularly active mature bucks may lose up to 20 percent -- or more -- of their body weight. They simply do not eat adequately during this time. After running and fasting, the bucks rest a few days then go into a feeding frenzy. Unfortunately for hunters, recent hunting pressure causes much of this feeding to occur after dark. In some areas of the North, deer tend to "yard-up." Look for deer, especially bucks, in areas offering sufficient food.

If the hunting season remains open during the post-rut period (as in many areas of the South) driving can be an excellent hunting method. But so can hunting near patches of honeysuckle, a favored late winter food in the South.

In general, hunting during the post-season is not unlike hunting during the difficult times of the pre-season. Primarily it means having to hunt food sources, natural or otherwise. The only difference is that the deer, especially the mature bucks, have just been through an entire hunting season and are extremely wary.

A fruitless hunt is better than no hunt

Some time ago I hunted in central Alabama with J. Wayne Fears, based out of his Cross Creek Hollow headquarters. It was late January before I had the opportunity to journey there, and the peak of the rut had been over about month.

The game plan was simple. With the rut already over we would hunt food sources. Deer sign in the form of tracks was abundant. Scrapes, however, were littered with leaves, having gone unchecked for at least a couple of weeks. Similarly, rubs were starting to gray from a lack of use. At one time, based on the sign, several bucks had been in the area. We hoped there still would be, now that the post-rut period was well underway.

After some quick scouting we found a couple of likely ridges. They stood next to areas of recently planted pines where the ground was covered with honeysuckle vines. The honeysuckle appeared to have

Whitetail live in a great variety of habitat. Sometimes the best place to find a mature buck is to look for them, where no one else does!

been browsed quite heavily during recent weeks. Several trails led to the honeysuckle. We would set up on one of the hillsides which commanded a view the honeysuckle, and with any luck we might ambush a buck as he came to feed.

That afternoon both Wayne and I sat where we could see different part of the honeysuckle patches. Just at dark the first deer started appearing in the tangle on the hillside, a couple of does, then a young eight point buck. At first I was tempted, my record of taking whitetails in Alabama having been rather poor. But the temptation passed as I watched the young buck hungrily feed on the honey-suckle. All the while I kept hoping a mature buck would appear. None did.

For the next four days Wayne and I maintained our vigil of the honeysuckle patches. We saw several deer, including two or three bucks that were tempting, but not quite what we were seeking.

During those days at Cross Creek Hollow we had a great hunt, cooked some outstanding meals, spent a lot of time visiting about previous hunts and hunts we planned to do in the future. When the hunt was over, the meat pole was still bare, but only in terms of deer and not in terms of a good time. After all, we had thoroughly enjoyed the hunt. Hunting the post-rut, therefore, is by no means easy, but it sure beats not hunting at all!

Chapter 11

Rattling

The peak of the rut was still at least two weeks away. What mature bucks I had seen apparently were much more interested in rubbing shrubs and trees, making scrapes, and sparring than they were in chasing does. Only the younger bucks were making runs at does. Their advances were met with stares of disdain and threats of physical violence.

Mature bucks, though plentiful on the property, were making themselves scarce. I suspected the fall shuffle was underway, when bucks started changing from their late summer routine and moving toward the breeding season. During the previous afternoon I had seen two bucks sparring near the spot I intended to hunt a little later in the morning.

The one that didn't get away

At present I sat watching a place where two trails converged, both of which led from one dense thicket to others. I intended to hunt the trails until about 9:00 that morning, then head to a similar area that the rancher's wife was hunting. Nothing showed on the trails, so as planned, I left and drove to where the woman waited.

She had seen nothing of interest and was ready to head back to camp. I suggested we try one more spot before doing so. A couple of weeks earlier I had seen a particularly large multi-tined buck near a thicket not far from camp. We drove to within 200 yards of the spot. I planned to "work" the horns, despite knowing that no self-respecting buck was supposed to come to horns this early in the season.Hoping to find a good buck for the woman to shoot, I left my rifle in the pickup -- an act I have mildly regretted.

We took our time easing into the thicket. Having hunted there before, I knew that inside the wall of thick brush the center of the thicket was relatively open. We quietly made our way to a spot where we could watch such an open area downwind of our position. In all likelihood if a buck responded, especially a mature buck, he would circle our position and approach from our downwind side. I had seen mature bucks behave that way many times.

We sat quietly for about 10 minutes, allowing the sounds of nature to return to normal. I then picked up one of my rattling horns and started vigorously rubbing a nearby juniper, while with the other I scratched the ground, to imitate a buck rubbing his antlers and pushing with his feet. I continued this for about a minute, then waited about another minute before bringing the two rattling horns together softly and timidly like two bucks sparring.

I had just started my sparring imitation when I noticed a buck moving toward us. It took only a brief look. At that moment I wished for my rifle, for the buck was one I had sought for several hunting seasons.

The rancher's wife already had her rifle pointed toward the deer. "Shoot!" I whispered. At the shot the buck went down, tried to recover and fell again. Even before we began walking toward the downed animal I knew this was a great deer, the kind I had long dreamed of taking.

The buck indeed was a true monster, a typical 14 point with seven extra-typical points over an inch long. His antlers' gross score exceeded Boone & Crockett's minimum of 195. However, when the net score was finally tallied the rack fell just below the minimum. He was a tremendous deer, at least nine years old.

The rut is THE time to use rattling horns.

The buck was and remains the biggest I have ever rattled up, and that actually was taken. (In essence it actually was rubbed up.) I have rattled up bigger bucks, but alas, they escaped unscathed.

The dubious origins of rattling

Horn rattling is essentially the imitation of two bucks fighting. An explanation of who first started the technique depends upon whom you talk to. In the Southwest we are told Mexican vaqueros started rattling up bucks back in the 1600s. If you are from the North, you will be told it was a technique developed by some long disappeared Indian tribe.

Regardless of where the technique was developed, for many years horn rattling was associated with hunting in Texas. It fact, it was widely believed that the technique would not work outside of Texas. Now, of course, we know differently, and nearly everywhere whitetails live, hunters are rattling up bucks. We also have seen the rise of many "experts" who claim their exact techniques are the only way to rattle -- if you want to be successful. I definitely am not one of those experts!

Determining who rattled up the first bucks to within atlatl, bow or possibly musket range is unimportant. What is important, however, is that the technique works -- at least some of the time.

Bill Whitfield rattles up a good buck in the deep sandy country of south Texas.

Why bucks fight — and why rattling works

Why do bucks respond to rattling, supposedly the sound of two bucks fighting? Some people claim bucks fight over does. Others believe they fight over territory. Personally, I think that bucks fighting over a doe seems a bit too romantic and probably is not a realistic evaluation of the bucks' motives.

Occasionally I have seen bucks that were following a doe get into a fight. This happens when one buck gets too close to another during the chase. Such fights generally are brief, lest they fall too far behind the doe. It also is not unusual for does to respond to buck fights. Some may come to investigate purely out of curiosity. Others may respond to see what bucks are fighting and if one is of interest to her. No one really knows for sure.

White-tailed bucks do tend to set up loose territories or core areas where they spend considerable time. However, they do not defend these as other territorial animals do. I often have observed two or three large, mature bucks living in the same area. Most hunters would consider any one of those bucks the "dominant" buck in the area, basing their judgment not only on appearance but also the buck's actions.

When bucks on the move travel through the core areas of other bucks, there occasionally are fights. Often these chance meetings are resolved simply by hard stares and body language, rather than fights. However if battles occur they can be serious, "I'm gonna kill you!" confrontations. However, I do not think fights between bucks are necessarily over territory. Sometimes they may simply be struggles for dominance, one buck trying to prove superiority over another.

Does fighting insure the survival of the fittest? Not necessarily. Quite often the best bucks -- both in antler and body -- get their antlers entangled with another buck (locked racks) and die a horrible death. Sometimes too, the strongest, best fighters do not get to do much breeding. To me, insuring the survival of the fittest through fighting is not necessarily important, because the true fittest might actually be the wariest -- those individuals that are smart rather than simply brawny.

I think the primary reason bucks fight during the fall is because of their high level of hormones, resulting in irritability. They think they are tough and are out to prove it. They remain in this highly irritable state throughout the majority of the rut. The higher a buck's state of irritability, the more aggressive he is going to be.

I have seen bucks in breeding pens fight even though there seemed no need to do so. Some of these bucks, with antlers sawed flush with their pedicels, got into fights with any buck that came too close, regardless of where such meetings occurred in a rather large pen.

I also have seen the changes that come over pet bucks as the rut approached. While they are in velvet, they were friendly and docile. After the velvet came off, however, they became aggressive and downright mean! Just before the peak of the rut they showed every intention of killing the hands that fed them. Fighting over does? I doubt it. Fighting over territory? I doubt it. Fighting over dominance? Perhaps. Fighting because they were irritable and mad at the world? I definitely think so!

Some bucks are good fighters, others are not. Those that are not, either learn quickly to avoid other bucks or continue getting whipped. Quite often the best and fiercest fighters are the big-bodied eight point bucks. Size of antlers really has nothing to do with a buck's ability to fight, or even his dominance. In some instances his large antlers might even be a detriment.

So again the question, why do bucks respond to the sound of other bucks fighting? I believe they respond out of curiosity, anxious to see what is going on. They also may respond out of a desire to get into a fight. If, by chance, the clashing bucks are fighting over a doe, some bucks might respond in order to steal off with the doe. To be honest, however, no one knows for certain why bucks respond to the sound of other bucks fighting.

I correlate bucks responding to horns with human behaviors. When a fight starts in a school playground or even in a bar, or for that matter at a ball game, people respond by running toward it. Why? Probably for the same reason bucks respond to rattling horns. Honestly, I do not really care why bucks respond. What I care about is that they do!

Bucks generally respond to rattling in a variety of ways. Some come charging in, their hair standing on end to make them look larger than they are. Some come in at a lope, while still others come slipping in cautiously. But there is one thing nearly all bucks which respond to rattling horns have in common: *they come in from the downwind side.* Initially they might approach the fight sounds from a different direction, but they most likely will circle and continue in from the downwind side. That is the primary reason for watching downwind.

Carolyn Williams with a buck she shot after the author rubbed him up, imitating a buck rubbing his antlers and barely meshing the tines together to imitate a pre-rut spar.

There are those "experts" who claim their ways of rattling are the only ways to be successful. I find such statements both erroneous and amusing! I have seen bucks rattled up with dried oak, juniper and mesquite sticks. I have seen bucks rattled up by tapping a pocket knife against a wooden rifle stock.

The most bizarre sound I ever have witnessed bucks responding to was the jaw-popping of a dying javelina (which sounded vaguely

144

like bucks fighting) in deep south Texas. In the latter instance I watched in amazement as five big mature bucks responded to the sound after I had shot the javelina. Obviously, when bucks are wanting to respond they will pursue almost any sound that resembles two bucks fighting.

There also are hunters who insist on using two left or two right side antlers when rattling. If that is the only method that works for them, great! As for me I prefer using left and right sides of a rack, preferably from a double-forked mule deer rack. These, *to me*, most closely imitate the sounds of two racks coming together, rather than sounding like a hunter rattling horns. This, of course, is simply my preference, based on years of trying to rattle up bucks from just south of the tundra in Canada into Mexico, and from the eastern slope of the Rockies to the Eastern Seaboard.

Real or synthetic, the choice is yours. The rattling horns I have used for the past several years are a pair of synthetics, cast from my favorite old set of mule deer rattling horns I used for several years. (These are marketed under the name of "Magnum Rattling Horns," available through P.O. Box 885, Uvalde, Texas 78802.) They are rather large, which I consider important because of the sound they make and because their louder sound carries farther. I can rattle these softly to make them sound like two bucks sparring, or loudly as of the bucks are trying to kill each other.

Rattling during the early rut

While there may no right or wrong way to rattle up a buck, you can increase your chances by trying to imitate what the deer are doing in the wild. In the early part of the rut, the bucks spend considerable time rubbing their antlers and timidly sparring. As the peak of the rut approaches the bucks are much more aggressive, fighting more intensely and much longer. As the ardor of the rut wanes, the fights occur less frequently and with less intensity. Trying to duplicate these changes will increase your chances of drawing bucks.

Rattling works anywhere there are whitetails. It works better where there is an abundance of bucks. The narrower the buck-to-doe ratio, the greater the chances of rattling in bucks. Is this because of greater competition between bucks for does? Maybe, but I think it is simply because there are more bucks in such herds. Thus, chances are greater that one or more bucks will respond.

At the beginning of this chapter I told of a buck that was rubbed up during the pre-rut period. Such use of rattling horns will often bring buck response when more intense rattling will not. Steve Warner and Bob Parker, Jr. are extremely good whitetail hunters. Steve, a veteran wildlife biologist, happens to work for Parker and also is the designer of Bushlan Camo. Bob is one of the best and most dedicated big-deer hunters with whom I have had the pleasure of sharing a hunting camp.

On their well-managed ranch Bob was hunting a huge deer that Steve had located in late summer. I had seen the deer while on a scouting trip the previous February. The deer appeared to be well worth the effort of spending whatever time was needed to take him.

They started hunting the buck about three weeks before the peak of the rut. First they tried sitting in areas where the buck reportedly had been seen. Then they tried still-hunting -- and any and everything else they could think of. Finally, Steve decided to hunt with Bob in the area where the buck supposedly lived.

During the early morning they watched an area of low-growing brush. The hunters were situated in a couple of tripods that provided a commanding view of the surrounding countryside. About 9:00 in the morning Steve crawled down and rubbed his rattling horns against a bush, intending to follow with a sparring sequence.

As soon as he started rubbing the brush three big bucks stood up within 200 yards of the stands. None of the bucks had been visible during the morning, even though both hunters had watched since before daylight, but when Steve started "hooking" the brush with his rattling horn the bucks stood up and stared in the direction of the racket.

One of the bucks was a huge typical 12 point. While it was not the monstrous buck Bob had been seeking, the basic 160 Boone & Crockett buck simply was too big to pass. Chalk up another buck, thanks to rubbing during the early season.

During their time of sparring, bucks gingerly bring their antlers together, push briefly and almost tentatively with minimal noise. They continue this for about 30 seconds, sometimes longer, sometimes shorter, then pull apart. Each then looks about for any other buck doing the same, and the sparring begins again. Such sparring matches seldom last more than two or three minutes.

I often have rattled up bucks during the early season by imitating these sparring matches. But as the peak of the rut approaches I normally change my rattling technique.

Rattling during the peak of the rut

As the rut approaches its peak and the bucks' hormones do the same, the intensity of the fights increases dramatically! What earlier were friendly sparring matches now turn into life and death confrontations. Anyone who thinks the contrary simply does not know, and has never seen a fight between two big, mature bucks trying to kill each other.

I have seen several such fights. Such struggles are accompanied by a great variety of noises, such as bucks pushing hard against each other; bucks pushing each other over brush, shrubs, or whatever gets in the way; and bucks flipping one another. The racket is unbelievable. No one truly duplicate the noise made by two big mature bucks fighting and trying to kill each other. But as the peak of the rut approaches, you should at least try to duplicate those sounds.

Bob Parker, Jr. admires the monstrous whitetail he and Steve Warner rubbed up during the pre-rut.

For the past few years I have served as a judge at the World Championship Deer Rattling and Calling Contest. Other judges of this event include: John Wootters, who needs no introduction to deer hunters; Bob Ramsey, whom many consider the father of horn rattling and who is responsible for introducing it to most of North America; Murray Burnham, of game calling fame; Dr. James Kroll, a prominent whitetail researcher, hunter and writer.

This group of judges agrees unanimously on one fact: Most contestants simply are too timid in their rattling techniques. This is especially evident because the contestants are told they are rattling during the peak of the rut. Most hunters fall into the same category. They simply do not make enough noise!

Maximize your noise

As with any rattling, during the peak of the rut it is best to rattle in areas where you think bucks exist, either because you have located buck sign or sighted bucks in the area. I like to rattle in the vicinity of several scrapes and rubs, in an area near some thick brush that still allows me to see a buck approaching. (It does no good to rattle up a buck that cannot be seen!)

When setting up to rattle during or near the peak of the rut, I find a place where I can watch downwind and where the camo I am wearing will blend in. When rattling, I fully camouflage from head to toe, including hands and face.

As a simple safety precaution, I set up far from any other hunting activity. I am fortunate to hunt in areas where there is little hunting pressure. If I hunted where a hunter was hiding behind every bush, I would not even think of rattling horns while other hunters were in the woods!

I also try to set up near a dried brush I can break, and rocks I can roll -- the more the better, because I want to make as much racket as possible. If my position does not have the requisite dried brush, I'll pull some over to where I intend to set up.

After the natural noises settle back to normal, I start by mimicking a couple of soft grunts, possibly a snort-wheeze. Then I bring the antlers together, softly at first and then increasing the noise. Grasping each antler tightly I bring them gingerly together and twist my wrists as I try to imitate two bucks pushing. I sometimes dig my heels into the ground to sound like two bucks pushing each other. At the same time I will kick nearby brush and slam the antlers into the dried brush and shrubs, then kick at loose brush and rocks to make them roll. As the "fight" continues, I wrench the antlers apart, then slam them together as loudly as I can. All the while I make as much noise as I possibly can.

If deer respond quickly I might rattle only a minute or two. Other times, when deer are responding slowly, I may rattle for 10 minutes. Buck fights are not timed like a boxing match, as some of the "experts" would have us believe. I have seen some fights last less than a minute. I have seen other fights that lasted as long as six hours! So dare to do things a little differently, especially if others in your area hunt with rattling horns.

During the entire time you rattle keep your gun handy -- a buck may respond at anytime, from the first clash of antlers until 20 to 30 minutes after you have quit rattling. Far too many hunters rattle for a while and then, if no deer appear immediately, move to another area to try again. If you hunt with rattling, be sure to stay in the same spot for at least 30 minutes after you quit, just in case an old mature deer is slow in responding. Quite often, older bucks are slow to investigate.

Rattling with patience

As the peak of the rut approaches it is, by far, my favorite time for rattling. But it requires patience. Don't shoot the first buck that responds unless it is the buck you really want to take. While taping a television show with Bill Jordan of Realtree Camouflage fame, David Blanton (the cameraman) and I were hunting with Bill Whitfield on the Encintos Ranch in Texas. At one setting we rattled up seven different bucks. The first were youngsters. The last two were good 10 point bucks. If hunting anywhere else, I would have squeezed a trigger on either of those last ones. But on that ranch there are some truly big bucks and I wanted a chance at one of the big boys. During the four days we filmed and hunted on the Encinitos, we rattled up approximately 30 different bucks. That was one of those trips where everything seemed to work.

The following year -- same time, same ranch, essentially the same weather -- we had difficulty rattling up even one buck. All to prove that sometimes rattling works, sometimes it does not. Success really depends upon the attitude of the bucks!

On still another occasion on the same ranch we rattled up some extremely good bucks that responded immediately. John Pflueger, my guide, rattled up a buck that came at a run from a distance of almost 500 yards. I shot the buck as he stopped 50 yards from me, directly in front of where John was seated in a tripod. The animal was a six-year-old 12 point with a 20-inch spread.

Yes, you can rattle bucks, including mature bucks, even when the person rattling the horns is up in the air. Rattling from above restricts a hunter from making as much noise as he could on the ground, but the technique occasionally works. So don't think you have to rattle from the ground. In certain instances rattling from a tree or tripod offers the definite advantage of seeing better and more territory.

The best buck I ever rattled up -- though it was not shot -- was near Tamaulipas, Mexico. We found an area near a dry creek bottom that had a great abundance of scrapes. I instructed my companion, Ron Davidson, an old friend and

The author with a mature whitetail buck, rattled up for him by guide John Pflueger.

dedicated whitetail hunter, to situate himself where he could see a couple of *senderos* downwind. I moved about 10 yards north of Ron, but only a few bushes separated the two of us.

After breaking brush and rattling for about five minutes I noticed movement *between* us. The buck was a monster, extremely massive, wide and tall, with numerous non-typical points. But there was little I could do. The buck was right between us. Moments later he was gone!

I later discovered Ron never saw the buck. The only place I saw the deer was when he stood exactly between the two of us. That buck did not stick around long. He was there and then gone! Always expect the unexpected -- forgetting to do so can cost you the deer of a lifetime.

The ideal time of day

The best time of the day to rattle? It seems to vary from day to day. On some days I have rattled up bucks all day long, while on other days only early in the morning or late in the afternoon. On other occasions I could not rattle up a buck regardless of the time of day. Sometimes rattling works best from about 11:00 a.m. until 2:00 or 3:00 p.m.

On one such occasion, Jay Gates and I were hunting a ranch with an abundance of bucks. From daylight until 11:00 a.m., we tried rattling at several promising places without attracting a single buck. Then at 11:00 it was as if someone had turned on a switch. From that moment until 1:30 in the afternoon we rattled up over 20 bucks! Several of those bucks were rattled from the very spots where nothing had responded earlier that day.

There is no greater thrill in whitetail hunting than when bucks respond to rattling horns near the peak of the rut. And there is not a more exciting way to take a big mature buck -- whether he comes sneaking in, warily looking for the bogus fight, or if he comes in with hair standing on end, eyes bugged, and ears laid back, ready to do battle. Each buck is exciting in his own way, whether you shoot or pass him.

And even if you do not rattle up a buck, do you know of any other hunting tactic that allows you to make as much noise as possible and still expect a deer to come? But through it all, remember that big bucks are different -- which brings up an interesting question.

Do truly big mature bucks respond to rattling horns? I think the answer is yes. Often, however, these bucks seem slow to respond. Mature bucks are a moody lot. Sometimes the older bucks respond, and on other days they do not, regardless of how realistic your imitated fight might be.

However, I think that sometimes the really big bucks respond readily, but because they do not move in closely the horn rattler may never see them. When hunting big mature bucks, therefore, it is a good idea to work with a trusted hunting partner. While either you or he rattles, have the other hunter move 20 to 50 yards. What is seen that far away from the rattler may surprise you.

Rattling after the peak of the rut

The peak of the intensive, aggressive rattling period lasts only a little longer than the peak of the rut. As the rut starts to wane, the number of serious fights decreases as well. In some ways the bucks still are going through the motions, and they are tiring of all the fighting. Buck fights, therefore, are less intense than only a few days before. To rattle up bucks during this time, make your fights sound realistic. The post rut fights are more intense than the pre-rut sparring matches, but they generally do not last as long as the fights did only a few days earlier.

I like to rattle late in the season near fresh rubs. The fresher the better. One year, my brother Glenn and I had the opportunity to hunt together about two weeks after the peak of the rut had finished. Uncertain we would be able to rattle up a buck, we nonetheless hoped.

I found a spot that simply "felt right." Glancing to my left I spotted a rub with sap still dripping from its edges. We set up hurriedly, and when Glenn was in position I immediately began rattling. As soon as I started meshing the antlers, a buck appeared about 20 yards away. My brother's aim was true and the deer was one of the best he has ever taken -- at least one of the most massive.

Doe decoys work great when rattling, however be sure the decoy is not staring in the horn rattler's direction.

Horn rattling is one of several techniques hunters of mature bucks have at their disposal. It is not the only method for taking a mature whitetail, but it certainly is one of the most exciting and fun! Your chances of rattling in bucks, especially mature bucks, can be greatly increased by hunting in areas with an abundance of bucks -- and by combining the technique with deer vocalizations, scents and even decoys. These will be discussed in the next chapter.

Chapter 12

Calling

He walked slowly in the stiff-legged manner typical of a rutting buck. With every few steps he made a grunting, almost pig-like sound. I had heard the sound, even before I saw the buck. At the time I assumed something was wrong with the deer. After all, everyone knew bucks did not make any noise.

A couple of weeks later, however, after the hunting season had opened, I was walking through the woods and just for the heck of it started making such a grunting sound. I continued doing so until I reached my deer stand, high in an ancient oak. When I reached the board seat nailed in the crotch of a couple of limbs, I look back along the trail I had come. There came a nice six point. Still in disbelief, I shot the buck as it walked toward my tree. I discounted the event as a fluke.

Not until seven years later, in 1969, did I again hear a white-tailed buck making grunting sounds. Actually, there were several bucks making grunts in our deer pens at Texas A&M University. When I mentioned this to several of the contemporary deer experts, they all laughed. Everyone knew deer did not make grunting sounds. Bleat, maybe, when then were young or in distress, but grunting? Never!

The next fall I started imitating the guttural grunting sounds I had heard bucks make during the breeding/hunting season. I grunted up several bucks. Unfortunately, it never occurred to me to build a call that might duplicate the sounds of a buck's grunt. Besides, I could closely duplicate those sounds with my mouth. Who needed a call....

The evolution of deer calls

Deer calling has come a long way since those days. Texas' Burnham Brothers were some of the early innovators of commercial deer calls. However, quite possibly the first grunt calls to appear on the market were those manufactured by Eli Haydel, a champion duck and goose caller from Louisiana. Haydel, also an accomplished musician, learned to duplicate the sounds of deer by listening to actual recordings.

Today, nearly any company producing a call lists a deer grunt call among its inventory. Whole companies have sprung up around the production of deer calls. Some of the calls closely duplicate the sounds made by deer, some do not. But in many instances it does not seem to matter, because deer are curious. Many people today will tell you how to call deer. Some truly know what they are talking about. Others simply are trying to sell calls, but even the latter seem to be effective.

Knowing how and when to use these deer calls can help you take a mature buck. Calls are not a cure-all, but they can be another tool in your bag of whitetail hunting tricks.

The sounds of bucks and does

As a wildlife biologist I have been involved in numerous deer research projects, involving both penned and free-roaming deer. I

Grunt calls are another tool the mature deer hunter should keep handy in his bag of tricks.

have had the opportunity to listen to and observe deer closely during the fall, specifically bucks during the three stages of the rut. My observations indicate that bucks tend to be most vocal during the fall breeding season.

On the other hand, does that I have observed have tended to be most vocal during the spring when fawns are at their sides. I am uncertain as to how vocal does are during the fall as their estrus cycles begin. Seldom have I heard does utter a sound during the fall, outside of the alarm snort, even when they are approaching the peak of their heat period.

However, several hunters have told me they have heard does make sounds that brought bucks to their sides. I have mimicked the sounds I was told they made, but without any success. I have made such sounds in areas with many bucks, both young and old. I have done the same where there were few bucks. Thus far I have been unable to attract a buck by using the sounds supposedly made by a doe coming into or already in estrus. However, I intend to keep trying.

In my opinion the best vocalizations to use during the fall are those made by the bucks, primarily the various grunts and the aggressive snort-wheeze. With these the caller will occasionally attract a mature buck.

Types of calls

During the early 1980s two major independent research projects, revolving around deer vocalizations, were conducted separately by Larry Richardson of Mississippi State University and by Thomas Atkeson at the University of Georgia. About 1984 many of deer grunt calls started hitting the market, as did a slew of deer calling experts.

Interestingly, Richardson distinguished eight type of calls. These included the bleat, nursing whine, foot stomp, distress call, alert-snort, the grunt, aggressive snort and the snort-wheeze.

Atkeson categorized five major calls, and a total of 12 variations. His five categories included: alarm calls including the snort and bawl; agonistic calls including low grunt, grunt-snort and the grunt-snort-wheeze; maternal/neonatal calls including maternal grunt, mew, bleat and nursing whine; mating calls including the tending grunt and flehmen-sniff; and contact calls.

While all these calls have a place at the right season, we are and should be primarily interested in imitating calls that typically are used during the fall. Of those mentioned, the call most of us hear most frequently is the alert snort, when deer either suspect, or see or smell danger. Deer use this call to alert other deer in the area.

Some biologists and hunters believe snorting back at deer that have sounded an alert snort actually tends to calm them. I tend to agree.

I have on occasion used a distress type sound when trying to duplicate an intense buck fight. Occasionally, bucks in the pitch of battle make a loud bawling sound, typical of the distress sound made by mature deer. Adding this type of a vocalization to an imitated buck fight can lend more authenticity to such a rattling sequence.

The fall vocalizations which should interest the mature-buck deer hunter are those associated with the mating game. According to Richardson's research, grunts are divided into dominant/subordinate and cohesive grunts. The former, which lasts less than one second, is meant to lure a dominant buck into your hunting area. The cohesive grunt, which lasts at least one second, is used as a "broadcast" sound. It was Richardson who found that subordinate bucks seemed more attracted by these slightly longer grunts, especially when given in a three-grunt series.

The flehmen-sniff is described as an unvoiced sound, associated with a buck lip-curling when a buck comes upon and sniffs a doe's urine. This sound can be imitated by making a sniffing sound by breathing through pinched nostrils.

The aggressive snort or grunt-snort, an intense series of two to six snorts either preceded or followed by a grunt, is a sound associated with bucks during sparring and during the breeding season. I have heard this call made by a mature buck when a younger buck came too close to him. The vocalization is generally associated with antler threats by the older buck.

The snort-wheeze is the most aggressive vocalization used by bucks. It consists of an utterance that sounds something like a guttural, "fit-fit-fit-ffffeeeeeee!" or two to three short, almost spitting grunts, followed by a long drawn out wheezing sound. The snort-wheeze generally is made by a dominant buck right before he charges another buck. This is a sound I often use in conjunction with my aggressive horn rattling, as the peak of the rut nears. I also have heard the victorious buck make this sound after an intense dominance battle. Occasionally I have heard a buck make a snort wheeze as he walked into a group of does, apparently to impress them.

When bucks actively chase does in estrus, in the bucks' typical head low to the ground posture, I have heard them make a tending grunt. This is essentially a short "eck" sound made with nearly every step. Young bucks in particular tend to make this sound with each step when chasing does.

I have heard bucks make a similar grunt, though not as frequently, when they walk stiff-legged through the woods. I assume the grunts are made to alert other bucks of their presence or to let does know a buck is in the area, in case they are interested. When other bucks approach this sound, various other aggressive grunts and vocalizations may follow.

In an article in *Deer & Deer Hunting* magazine, C.J. Winand reported comparing the sounds made by various commercial grunt calls to actual grunts made by deer. Through the use of sophisticated equipment he discovered little difference among the grunts made with various commercial grunt calls. He also found little difference between the sounds of the commercial grunt calls and the grunts made by live deer!

Winand also conducted three years of field research, trying to attract live deer with various calls. He and his team came up with the same results, completely independent of each other. The best results were achieved by calls that were a bit higher pitched than the calls of live deer. Young and old mature bucks alike responded best to the higher pitched grunts.

The author with a fine Kentucky whitetail taken while hunting with calling greats Davie Hale and Harold Knight.

Using grunt calls

I have used grunt calls in a variety of ways. As the opening of this chapter suggests, I often have still-hunted my way to a stand or rattling spot, all the while grunting like a rut-crazed buck walking through the woods. Several times, long before reaching my destination, I have grunted up a buck by using this method.

I also have used a grunt tube frequently while hunting from a tripod in a likely buck area. I believe deer respond to these "blind" grunts as much out of curiosity as out of defense of the area or the promise or threat of a fight. I have grunted up several bucks while sitting in a tripod near several rubs and scrapes. These bucks have approached by slipping in, cautiously looking for the source of the grunts. When they appeared, I would shut up. As they started to leave I would again grunt softly.

Quite often I'll use various grunts in conjunction with rattling. Before starting a rattling sequence, or while rubbing a nearby bush, I will softly grunt two or three "ecks" occasionally. Then, while really meshing the horns, I may utter a deep, guttural "aaaaccckkkkk" -- like a buck really trying to muster energy to whip his opponent. Sometimes this brings in bucks that might otherwise hang back in the bushes and never show themselves. The same can be said for using the snort-wheeze. These are natural sounds associated with aggressive behavior, yet not many who rattle horns use them.

While on a hunt with Bill Whitfield, we spent an evening around a campfire talking about calling in big whitetails. I told Bill how to make and use the snort-wheeze call and suggested he try it, if the occasion arose where he thought its use might be proper.

The following morning Bill sat in a tripod overlooking a thicket. As he watched two bucks near a scrape, a third and much bigger

Harold Knight approaches a huge Kentucky whitetail he called to within shooting range.

buck momentarily appeared at the edge of the thicket, but before Bill could react the buck disappeared. At first Bill simply sat there not sure what to do. But then he remembered my instructions for the snort-wheeze.

Bill, as he tells it, began to make the vocalization, then thought about how silly he would sound. But after looking around to be sure no one was watching he decided to make the sound. He uttered forth a hissing, "fit-fit-fit-ffffeeeeeee." Just as quickly as he did the big mature buck came charging out of the thicket and strode toward the sound. This time Bill was ready.

In the mid-1970s I was hunting for a particularly large buck, especially large for the area where he lived. I had seen him several times, but each time he had given me the slip. The buck became an obsessive goal.

Hunting season had been open many days when I grabbed my rattling horns and headed to the edge of a thicket where I had seen him in the past. Setting up where he would have to move into an open area -- if he indeed responded -- I started my rattling sequence slowly, then increased the intensity. After rattling and beating the brush for a couple of minutes I saw movement at the edge of the brush. But try as I may, no amount of rattling would entice him out of the brush. I was at wit's end.

Then I started grunting. Immediately the buck burst out of the brush and charged toward me. Thankfully, I recovered in time. Had I not started grunting, the buck probably never would have given me a shot.

Too close for comfort

Several times I have held a buck's attention by grunting to him. On one such occasion the hunter with me was anxious to take a good buck, but he also wanted to film a buck coming to horns. The property we were hunting was managed to produce an abundance of mature bucks, and the timing was perfect to rattle up bucks. The rut was just about to jump into high gear. A cool front had passed through the day before and blown itself out, so only a slight breeze blew out of the north. The temperature was in the thirties making it feel like deer hunting weather.

My companion and I headed to an area where I previously had seen several big bucks. I instructed him to crawl up the tripod I had placed in the area the evening before. After things started to settle down I began rattling.

Very soon a good buck appeared, one with eight basic points and several non-typical points around the bases. The buck stopped about thirty yards away, staring directly at me. I was camouflaged from head to toe.

I looked up at the hunter -- he was looking in the wrong direction. The deer started to leave so I tickled the horns again. Immediately the buck turned back. This time he came to within about 20 steps of where I sat with my back against a bush.

Just then the hunter saw the deer and drew an audible deep breath. The buck spooked at the sound. I immediately started making soft grunts with my mouth. The buck again turned and then walked to within 10 feet of me. For the next 10 minutes, each time the buck turned to walk away I repeated the grunting routine.

Finally the buck stood fewer than 4 feet from me. His eyes were bugged, the hair on his back stood on end, his ears were laid back in a threatening manner. I began wondering what I was to do if the buck came any closer. Just when it appeared I would have to stand up and shout, or do something else to get rid of the buck, he obviously tired of the game, turned and walked away. This time I did not grunt as he left! Certainly the guy in the tripod had gained all kinds of fantastic footage.

I looked up at my companion and saw him just sitting there, the camera and his rifle lying on his lap. He later admitted being so enthralled with the drama that he completely forgot about either running the camera or taking a shot at the buck!

The buck that kept returning

On another occasion I spotted a buck walking down a trail. He was a nice 10 point with about a 19-inch spread. The hunter I had with me (this during my outfitter/guide days) quickly was instructed to sit by my side and get a steady rest. I started grunting a slow series of soft "eck" sounds.

David Knight blows softly on a grunt call to imitate the sounds of a buck tending a doe.

As soon as I began calling, the buck turned and walked directly toward us. At about 15 steps he stopped broadside. I looked over at my hunter. He was shaking vigorously, the end of the rifle barrel doing huge figure eights. As I tried to calm him with soft whispers he fired. The deer immediately ran off.

As the hunter ejected his spent cartridge and bolted in another round, I started grunting at the buck. Just that quickly the buck was back. The hunter shot at him a second time and missed. Again the buck disappeared and I started grunting again. The buck came back. And just as before, the hunter missed -- his third shot.

I started grunting immediately after the shot and within 10 seconds the buck again returned. As the hunter prepared to take another shot I reached up, grabbed the rifle and said aloud, "Three strikes and you're out!" The buck left in quite a hurry!

I shook my head and told the hunter we could do better. He was skeptical, but later that day I found him a better buck. The deer was about a hundred yards away, and not in his lap. This time his aim was true.

Other applications of the grunt call

Grunt calls are effective in other situations as well. Quite often I have enticed a buck out of the brush with a deer grunt. On several occasions, simply by blowing a little louder than usual on a grunt call, I have stopped bucks that seemed intent on going elsewhere. In most instances, when a buck hears a loud grunt he will stop. He might not respond by turning around, but at least he will stop long enough so I can quickly evaluate his age and antlers.

On other occasions, when does that were feeding around me became excited for no apparent reason, I have been able to calm simply by grunting softly. The soft grunts seemed to reassure them that nothing was wrong. While this grunting might not entice a buck to come, the presence of does means bucks may well come to investigate.

Grunt calls, regardless of whether you use a commercially manufactured call or your natural voice, can help you see and take mature bucks.

Chapter 13

Common Sense Scents

Of the mature buck's primary senses of sight, hearing and smell, he seems to rely quite heavily for his protection on his sense of smell. He has the ability to take in a myriad of odors and single out one or two that might forecast danger, or for that matter, potential pleasure. To a great extent, the mature buck depends on his sense of smell to determine the sexual status of does in his area.

To escape the detection of the buck's eyes, we can wear camouflage clothing (where it is legal) that blends in perfectly with the backgrounds where we hunt. Some areas now require the wearing of blaze orange, or at least a certain amount of blaze orange. In either case it is imperative to move slowly to further avoid detection.

To counteract the buck's sense of hearing we can sit or move quietly. We also can wear camouflage or other clothing made of various soft material such as wool blends, chamois cloth, fleece and other materials. These are soft to the touch and thus extremely quiet. These materials also can keep us comfortable in a variety of weather conditions.

Staying scent-free

Counteracting the human odor takes a bit more doing, as does using non-human scents. Basically two types of scents or lures are available to hunters hoping to take a mature buck. Perhaps the most important is the cover scent, which hopefully will counteract or mask human odor. The other is a scent or lure that attracts a deer to its location.

On the way to hunting camp and while in camp, we and our clothes come in contact with a tremendous variety of odors. It begins when the clothes are laundered. Perfumes in the laundry soap make them smell good to us, but may be like waving a flag at a deer. In addition, brighteners used in laundry soaps and dyes enhance a deer's ability to see these colors. (Recent research has demonstrated deer can see a much broader spectrum of colors than previously claimed, and that they can see certain ultra-violet colors we cannot see.) Thus, for starters, it is a good idea to wash hunting clothes separately with the new laundry products that both counteract odors and subdue the ultra-violet reflection of the fabrics.

I strive to avoid tainting the clothes with unnatural odors. To do this I avoid wearing my hunting clothes when en route to a hunting camp. I also don't wear them in camp where are people are cooking, or possibly smoking. When not wearing my hunting clothes I keep them in a plastic bag, to which I add foliage such as pine needles if I am hunting among pine, or juniper if juniper grows in the area I'll be hunting.

Bow hunters have learned much about remaining "squeaky clean" while hunting, and hunters of mature deer can learn much from them. In the past, I managed a couple of bow hunting operations in Texas where daytime temperatures in the fall can be downright warm. During the bow hunters' stay in camp the water heater ran constantly, primarily because the hunters all showered before the morning hunt, showered again before the afternoon hunt, then showered once more at night. Each person averaged three showers a day. When bathing they reduced the potential of human odor by using non-scented soaps, then followed their showers with non-scented deodorants.

The only time those hunters wore their camouflage hunting clothes was when they were hunting. They used a variety of human scent masking chemicals, and a fair amount of baking soda on clothes and in boots. Whenever someone thought his hunting clothes had become tainted with perspiration, he changed to another outfit. Each of us could learn much from spending a few days in camp with a group of such dedicated whitetail bow hunters.

Masking scents

Today there are many different masking scents on the market that counteract the human odors. Although I have used only a few, they seemed to work well. Friends who use such products swear by them.

I use the scents occasionally but tend to rely on natural scents from the area I am hunting, or strong-smelling urine based scents from animals native to the area. One of my favorite urine based cover scents comes from the raccoon. This animal is found through most, if not all, of the white-tailed deer's range. Raccoons do not present a danger to deer and thus signs of their presence are acceptable to deer. The same is generally true for fox urine.

Some hunters swear by bobcat, coyote, or skunk based scents. J. Wayne Fears, a whitetail hunter/biologist for whom I have utmost respect, has had great success using bobcat scent and actually has seen deer trailing him (after he had applied it to his shoes), probably to find where the predator had gone.

I tend to like scents that are natural and that do not present a threat or a sign of danger to the deer. I use these scents on the bottom of my boots, and also sprinkle them a little distance downwind of where I will be hunting.

Using local scents

I also like to use natural scents from plants in the area I am hunting. In most regions of the country there are highly aromatic plants that can be used as a cover scent. I already have mentioned using pine needles and juniper. Not only will I store my clothing with them, but when I leave camp I liberally rub such plant material on my clothing. When I find a spot from which to hunt, I again do the same. Both pine and juniper are found throughout much of the whitetail's range.

Natural cover scents such as rabbit tobacco work great to cover the human odor.

I also use a plant which J. Wayne Fears introduced me to while hunting in Alabama. Though it goes by various names, in many areas the plant is called rabbit tobacco. In other regions it may be called poverty weed, cudweed, catfoot, and old field balsam. The mountain men used this plant as a cover scent, carrying small balls made from the leaves in their pockets, or attached to their hat bands.

Apples, where they naturally exist, also provide a good natural cover scent. However, such a scent would do you little good if hunting where apples were not an everyday odor, such as in the arid Southwest.

One of the best natural cover scents I have found in such arid brush land is lantana. This low-growing shrub is extremely aromatic.

Always try to match your cover scent to something the local deer are familiar with. When hunting in cattle country, whether beef or dairy, I make it a point to step in fresh cow manure occasionally. This odor is one with which the deer are familiar.

Commercial cover scents

The natural scents I have mentioned work extremely well, and are free for the taking or using -- with the possible exception of the urine based scents. However, there also are various commercial cover scents that supposedly not only remove human odors from your body and clothing, but also cover or remove other odors. Remember, however, always to match your cover scent to the area you are hunting. Otherwise, you may be defeating the purpose of using a cover scent in the first place!

Attractor scents

Most attractor scents consist of a urine base. There are, however, some attractor scents made to smell like favored deer food, such as apples, corn and acorns. But generally, when we think of attractor scents, we think of the urine based scents from does or bucks.

Through many years I have tried a considerable number of attractant scents, from those made of doe-in-estrus urine, to scents from dominant bucks, to various heat-activated scents and candles, to gels, to wafers impregnated with doe-in-heat scents. I even have used fresh tarsal glands from recently taken bucks and does. I have tried a variety of home-made scents and nearly all the commercially produced scents.

On some days it seemed the deer, young and old, showed great interest in scents. On other days they avoided the odors. On those days when some of the bucks showed interest, others either avoided the scents or, at best, paid them little attention. As I already have contended, deer are individuals -- even in their reactions to scents.

Ranches I have managed have served me well as research areas. When the deer were being hunted, either by commercial hunters on guided hunts, or by families of the owners, I often used the hunters to try various products, to see what result they get with attractor scents. The products were tested well before the rut started, as the rut began, as the rut peaked, and after the rut was finished.

No matter which products we tried, the results were the same. Some deer on some days would go "hog wild" over the scents. On those same days, other deer seemingly couldn't care less about the scents being there. Admittedly, these properties are not average hunting areas. They boast extremely narrow buck-to-doe ratios, with an abundance of mature bucks within their herds. This may, in some way, bias the results.

I have seen people react to scents the same way as deer react. Once, while attending a sports show, I performed an informal experiment. On a long table that many people passed, I set out three film canisters. In one I put a sweet smelling perfume, in another I put some doe-in-heat scent, in the third a bit of dog feces. Some people were attracted to one of the three scents. Others completely avoided the area when they smelled one of the odors.

Deer seem to react the same way. I never have seen deer consistently attracted to any particular attractant scent. As mentioned, on some days they seem totally enthralled by the scents, on other days they couldn't care less.

The next observation may seem rather crude, but it does reinforce the point I am making. During the years when we had a considerable number of bucks in the pens at Texas A&M, least one or two female lab technicians would be working with the Wildlife Disease Project. Almost always, we could discern the woman's "time of the month" simply by the bucks' reactions when she walked into a deer pen. Most bucks immediately became nervous and began pacing back and forth. They became more irritable, but after the woman had left, they would return to normal. They immediately seemed to know.

On those same days, however, some bucks seemed unaffected by the woman's presence. I suspect the same phenomenon occurs in the wild, when bucks encounter doe-in-heat urine placed there as a lure. Could it be that deer too are moody and temperamental?

From my perspective as a biologist, the importance of using attractant scents seems only somewhat important. Their most important effect may be psychological -- on the hunter. If a hunter uses an attractant scent, he will expect to see a deer or have something spectacular happen. Therefore, the hunter is much more observant of what is going on around him. When a deer appears, he sees it. I have seen hunters miss seeing deer, because they were thinking of things other than hunting, such as their relationships with others, business matters and the like. As I emphasized in chapter seven, the key to seeing deer is expecting to see them.

As mentioned before, when I was a youngster my dad used to leave me at my stand before continuing on to his. His parting words were always the same: "Be awoke, son!" This, of course, was his way of reminding me not to daydream, but to pay attention to what was going on around me, to keep a keen lookout for deer and any signs that could help me see deer. It was extremely good advice then and still is today. Hunting mature deer is not only a physical game, it is a mental game. And at times it seems much more mental than anything else. Thus, if using attractant scents can help you "be awoke," by all means do so!

I use cover scents quite often, and attractant scents -- especially the doe in heat or dominant buck (including fresh and frozen tarsal glands) -- while rattling and to "sweeten" scrapes. These scents often will cause a mature buck to visit a scrape more frequently than normal. When setting up to rattle I sprinkle attractant scents in two or three places, or set out film canisters that contain the scents, just beyond where I intend to hide. I also use them in conjunction with doe decoys while rattling.

The doe decoy is set out where an approaching buck can see her. I douse the decoy with doe-in-heat scent. When a buck approaches he concentrates on her rather than on me. I have successfully used this method numerous times. I also have used the doe-in-heat scent with stationary decoys placed where deer can see them from a distance.

Researchers are learning more and more about the role of scents in whitetail communication and will likely continue doing so in the future. Volumes could be written about deer scents marking rubs and scrapes. But here, from a practical aspect, why they do such things is not so important as simply that they do!

The author with a good whitetail taken with Thompson/Center Contender while using attractant scents to lure the buck to his hunting area.

166

Chapter 14

Decoying Deer

Poachers had been slipping across our property lines and shooting deer. To catch them in the act, I built a styrofoam deer decoy, making it life-like as possible, right down to a fair-sized rack. I placed it in an area where I could watch the decoy in case someone shot at it. By the time I had finished setting it up, night had fallen.

The next morning I returned before daylight, and the glow of the flashlight I saw my decoy had been knocked over and the grass around trampled. Aggravated, I set it back up. The following morning I went back to the decoy. This time I found it in pieces.

At first convinced the poachers had come after dark and destroyed my decoy, I then noticed punctures in the decoy's body -- lots of them! I also saw a few deer tracks. Gradually I pieced together the mystery. During the night one or more live white-tailed bucks had "visited" the decoy and literally destroyed it!

That was back in the middle 1960s. A few years later a local game warden and I (at the time I was occasionally doing some wildlife forensic work with game wardens of the state) used similar decoys to catch poachers. Unfortunately the judges at the time declared our tactics "entrapment" and the cases were dismissed. After being told not to use decoys to catch poachers I quit messing with them. But things changed. Almost 30 years later I started using deer decoys while hunting.

Early experiments

During the early 1970s I started using homemade papier-mache' turkey decoys in conjunction with deer hunting. (This was before turkey decoys became popular and readily available as they are now.) I used the turkey decoys as confidence decoys. The area I hunted had a fair number of wild turkeys, and I noticed that when turkeys were in the larger food plots, deer usually seemed less wary. Thus, I started setting up turkey decoys in the fields during the fall. Several of the bow hunters on our archery hunts took deer while turkey decoys were in the green fields. Even today, we occasionally use turkey decoys for this purpose on some of the ranches I manage.

Decoying deer is not really anything new. Some evidence indicates that early inhabitants of North America may have used deer decoys to entice deer within range for hundreds of years. However, the practice has once again gained great acceptance and popularity with the introduction of lightweight, truly lifelike decoys manufactured by Feather-Flex, Flambeau, Montana Critters and others.

Using decoys

If you plan on hunting with a deer decoy it is best done where there is little or no other hunting pressure, such as on private land where you know who is hunting with you and where they are hunting. I would never use a deer decoy while hunting on public land, or where there is any amount of hunting pressure. Not only could sitting anywhere near a decoy be dangerous, so could carrying it in and out of the woods. Even when hunting on private property, I try to spray blaze orange on the decoy where the deer normally would be white. Some scientific evidence shows that deer tend to perceive blaze orange as white. Thus, while the deer see white, fellow hunters see blaze orange.

As to using buck or doe decoys, I have had more experience with doe decoys, either those that stand up or those lying down with heads erect. When setting up such decoys, I place them where they can be seen by deer, such as along trails, on the edge of natural openings or fields, or, in conjunction with rattling, in a readily visible spot.

Do not set out a decoy and leave it for any length of time, lest deer become accustomed to its presence and pay it little attention. Also, do not start using the decoy too early in the season. Generally where hunting seasons encompass the rut, the seasons open much earlier. Do not use a decoy so much that the local deer grow accustomed to it.

Decoy placement

As already mentioned, when setting up a decoy place it where both any approaching deer and you can see it -- at a distance that will offer you a good shot. However, always set the decoy, whether buck or doe, so it is not looking in your direction. Avoid giving the impression the decoy is staring at something near where you are hidden.

Set the decoy up where it is essentially facing into the wind, because that is the way deer usually move or approach anything. You might consider setting the decoy next to a fallen tree, log or dense underbrush, so when a buck approaches the decoy he is forced to offer you a broadside shot.

There are advantages to using either a standing decoy or a lying down one. A standing decoy is more visible and should be more readily seen. A lying down decoy may convey one of two messages. First, it may communicate a relaxed attitude, and deer feel a bit more comfortable about their location when they see this.

Second (if it is a doe decoy), it may imply that she has recently been bred. However, that does not necessarily mean she no longer is interested in further attention from a buck. Deer expect little movement from a another deer that is lying down. Therefore bucks, especially those that respond to rattling horns, generally will walk over and investigate the lying down, head erect decoy to see if she is still interested in sexual activities.

Guide John Pflueger sets up a doe decoy near where he and his hunter will be rattling and spending the afternoon.

Decoy "tricks"

During the rut a decoy can be doused with doe-in-heat scent. The scent with which I have had the most consistent success is Get-a-Buck, produced in Texas, which uses nothing but actual urine taken from does during their estrus cycle.

Generally, I trickle small amounts of the doe-in-heat scent along what might have been the trail my decoy would have taken to where she is standing. Then I'll sprinkle a liberal amount on the decoy itself, especially on the backside. Some decoys come equipped with real deer tails that allow for some movement. On decoys that do not, you can easily attach a rag or paper towel where the tail would be and then add scent to the make-believe tail.

You can get even more imaginative when hunting over a deer decoy. I have watched Bill Jordan (of Realtree fame) attach a rag to a doe decoy's tail, douse it with doe-in-heat scent, then tie a length of monofilament fishing line to the tail. By occasionally tugging the fishing line from his hiding place, Bill could make the tail twitch in a manner similar to that of a real doe. According to Bill, on several occasions he has used this trick to keep a buck's attention for quite some time, and occasionally enticed a buck to come for a closer look. I have witnessed Bill make a mature buck come closer, simply by making the doe decoy's tail twitch!

Decoys and rattling

I have had excellent success with buck and doe decoys when rattling. The primary purpose of these decoys is simply to hold their attention. I am convinced that decoys have drawn some bucks out of the brush that otherwise might never have shown themselves.

On one such occasion I was set up in an area not far from a brushy creek bottom. Vegetation was primarily willows, cattails, and shrubs that looked similar to tamaracks. Next to the creek was a fairly small opening. That day I carried a Feather-Flex lying down doe decoy, primarily because it folds up into a small package and can be carried in a large fleece Fieldline daypack. I hurriedly set the doe decoy so it appeared to be looking into the dense creek bottom, then positioned myself a short distance behind her and started rattling.

Although nothing appeared at first, I felt particularly good about the area, especially because I thought I had smelled the musky odor of a rutting buck. Just as I was beginning to doubt my choice of a spot, a movement just inside the creek bottom caught my eye. Next I saw an antler barely protruding from a thicket. The buck was looking intently at the decoy.

Moments later the buck moved slightly forward, exposing just enough of his shoulder for me to make the shot. I doubt the old buck would have given me the shot, had it not been for the decoy to draw him out of the brush.

Setting up during the rut

When using doe decoys enhanced with a fair amount of doe-in-heat-scent or urine, I have observed that other does tend to avoid the decoys. However, I also have seen the same happen with live deer. When a doe comes into heat, other does avoid her. Why this occurs, or even if this is a universal occurrence, I do not know.

In setting up doe decoys during the rut, I tend to set them up where I expect to see bucks and near where exists at least a fair amount of buck sign, such as rubs and scrapes. The results can be spectacular.

On one such occasion I used a doe decoy on the edge of an old overgrown field. Along the field's edges were several scrapes frequented by no less than three mature bucks. (I had seen the bucks from a distance, and thus knew of their presence in the area.) A few days before the peak of the rut, I placed the doe decoy into the area. Then, dragging behind me a rag soaked with Get-a-Buck doe-in-heat urine, I made a couple of paths across the field and just into the edge of the woods. My scent trail completed, I attached the scented rag to the decoy's tail. I then crawled into a tree that provided me a great vantage point, and waited.

The afternoon was cool with a wind out of the northeast. Just before dark the first buck appeared, caught the scent and started trailing in typical head-to-the-ground rutting behavior. When he spotted the doe he headed directly toward her, then started circling her, getting closer with each pass. He finally approached her from the rear, smelled of the tail and tried to mount her, knocking the decoy to the ground. At that point he looked around briefly and walked back into the woods.

Hunter Bret Triplett with a good buck taken as it came to investigate a decoy set out, while also rattling and grunting.

As soon as he was gone I crawled down, set the decoy in an upright position, then crawled back up to my perch. I did not have to wait long. Another buck entered the field, briefly checked a scrape and then spotted the doe. He boldly walked toward her. He smelled of her head and circled around her, sniffing and looking closely as he moved. When she did not move he walked behind her and began goring her with his horns. When the decoy fell, he too ran off. By then it was getting too dark to see, so I packed up my decoy and headed to camp.

Both bucks had been at least three year olds, one with a very interesting 10 point rack and the other with a massive, though narrow, eight point rack. Had I chosen to do so, I could have taken either one of the bucks at nearly any time it was near the decoy.

Of course, using a deer decoy does not guarantee this kind of non-stop action. On many occasions I have seen bucks pay no attention at all to a doe decoy, or at least none that I could detect.

Some hunters prefer to use buck decoys in conjunction with hunting near rubs and scrapes. They have reported a variety of interesting behavior, including bucks goring buck decoys. The current crop of buck decoys looks extremely realistic. I therefore am reluctant to use or recommend the use of a buck decoy, primarily because it can be unsafe to hunt near one or carry it through the woods.

Although deer decoying has been around for centuries, we are still learning. Will using a deer decoy insure your chances of taking a mature buck? Maybe, maybe not. But, like using rattling horns, calls and scents, deer decoys are tools of the trade for those of us who hunt mature bucks.

Chapter 15

Food Plot Strategies

The search for food, even by mature bucks, is a primary driving impulse for survival. This is especially true during the early autumn and after the peak of the rut. All deer, especially bucks, are ravenously hungry during the early fall as they prepare for the activities of the breeding season. After the rut is over, bucks try to replenish their body reserves used during the rigors of the breeding season, not only to restore body condition, but also to get ready for the next round of antler development.

Yet, even during the rut, bucks seek out highly nutritious food to carry them through the lean days of actively chasing does. Bucks also know if they find ready food sources, does will be there -- or at least close by.

For years, farmers have known -- and often complained -- that deer will eat a lot of agricultural crops, and that the animals flourish on these highly nutritional forages. In certain areas of such range crops, depredation by deer is a serious problem. Hunting around these agricultural areas, near fields planted in corn, soybeans, or forage crops such as alfalfa (and a great variety of other crops) can prove highly successful. Hunters and deer managers have learned much from the experience of farmers.

Food plots that enhance hunting

These days many deer managers plan food plots specifically for deer forage. In order for deer to be healthy and do their best they should be on a high quality diet throughout the year, including during the late winter. In a natural state, late winter is a time of nutritional value in plants, with the exception of some legumes such

Glenn Weishuhn checks a food plot, planted strictly for forage for deer.

as alfalfa and winter cereal crops, such as wheat, oats and rye. Thus, managers have learned to plant deer forage crops that grow and produce well during the late fall and winter. Each year more food plots are being planted where previously there were none.

Deer adjust to these fields of forage in only a short time. How far they will travel to an individual field is hard to estimate, and probably depends upon how far the local deer normally travel for food. In areas where they normally do not travel very far, they likely will not travel far to use a food plot. However, where deer travel quite a distance under normal conditions, they likely will do the same to use food plots. In either case, when setting up food plots as part of a management program it is far better to plant numerous small fields than one or two large ones.

Hunting food plots successfully

As more hunting areas use food plots, learning to hunt them will become increasingly important. In some areas hunters have been hunting around food plots for many years. In other areas food plot hunting is just now starting, both deer and hunters will require some time to adapt.

Early in the fall, before there is any appreciable hunting pressure, even mature deer will frequent food plots during daylight hours. I recommend setting up a blind near where a trail ends in the field, where you can see the last few feet of the trail and the majority of the food plot. Such an area generally is a hot spot during the archery season, and sometimes even during the beginning of the firearms season.

While food plots may have permanent blinds built on them (this is mostly the case in the South and Southwest), it is a better idea to use a tripod, ladder stand, or climber. This will allow you to move around if deer quit using one trail and shift to another.

In most cases, mature does and bucks tend to avoid fields where permanent blinds are prominently displayed. I know there are exceptions to this, for I also have hunted in areas with permanent stands that consistently produce mature deer. However, these are truly exceptions.

Hunting around food plots can pay big dividends, if you know how to hunt them properly.

Hunting in the evening

As the hunting season progresses and deer become more wary, (especially about feeding in food plots and open fields) and bucks start thinking seriously about does, it is time to change hunting tactics. We all know that, while deer still feed in green fields or food plots, mature bucks tend to use the fields only after dark. Right? Maybe.

While it is wise to assume mature bucks frequent these food plots only at night or late in the afternoon, mature bucks occasionally will feed in food plots during the middle of the day. I have seen this happen on several occasions, especially when such feeding areas have had someone hunting on them early and late. Therefore, I advise occasionally checking these food plots during a midday hunt.

After hunting food plots for many years, I have concluded that deer tend to use them much more in the evening than the morning. Skipper Bettis, who manages the Sanctuary in Michigan, has made the same observation, including early in the season.

While with Skipper on the Sanctuary, we hunted food plots late in the afternoon. Each afternoon we watched bucks and does head toward a field, then hang up on the edges, waiting until nearly dark before entering to feed. By dark the fields had an abundance of deer. Those same fields were devoid of deer in the early mornings. This behavior seems to occur wherever I hunt around food plots, from Wyoming to Georgia, and Mexico to Saskatchewan, Canada.

One of my best deer was taken as it fed in a food plot late one afternoon on Jay Timmins's Doudle Creek Ranch near Brownwood. Bucks were just beginning to think about does. And even though the season had been open for a couple of weeks no one had hunted the property. The deer still were streaming into the field late in the afternoon.

*Bill Bynum, a field editor for **Deer & Deer Hunting**, checks for tracks leading to an agriculutural field, before deciding where to set up his tripod.*

The afternoon I spent there afforded an interesting lesson in deer behavior. Does came to feed on the lush wheat planted there. Bucks came to check on does. If a buck found one interested in his advances, the two quickly disappeared into the nearby brush. Sometimes several bucks followed the same doe.

Just before dark a wide, tall-tined buck entered the field. After careful evaluation, my guide suggested I shoot the buck, which I did. The buck remains one of my biggest and favorite bucks I have taken. At the Doudle Creek Ranch I hunted right next to the field. Had there been any appreciable previous hunting pressure I would have hunted trails leading to the fields.

Once the season gets under way bucks still frequent such food plots and green fields, but not in the same way they did a few weeks earlier. On many occasions I have seen a buck "hang up" on a trail leading to a field. Here he can check any doe that passes on her way to feed, then continue doing so until he finds a doe interested in his sexual advances or until it gets dark. Under the cover of darkness the buck enters the field to feed briefly and check out the rest of the does in the food plot. After dark, several bucks may be in the field doing the same. Unfortunately, by then it is past legal shooting hours.

A much better way to hunt these evening food plot bucks is to walk back into the woods and brush, back-tracking trails to where two or more converge. Look also for tracks and sign where a buck might have been waiting to check does traveling these trails. Find a tree to which you can attach a climber or ladder stand, or a spot where a tripod will allow you to watch the trails or "staging" areas. Then move your blind into the area during midday and prepare to hunt it that afternoon. (Normally such staging areas are from 50 to well over 100 yards from the edge of the field.)

Using this technique I have taken several good bucks, as well as put other hunters in the right areas for opportunities at such bucks. The first time J. Wayne Fears and I hunted together for whitetails we were on property I had been managing for about three years. Scattered throughout the acreage were several food plots of oats, wheat or alfalfa to provide deer with quality forage.

By the time Wayne arrived, the peak of the breeding season was just about over, rutting activity was starting to slow. We tried rattling, but few bucks responded. In the afternoons we hunted deer trails leading to the green fields.

As the season progresses, the best place to hunt a food plot is on trails leading to it, back off in the woods.

The first afternoon Wayne took an old mature deer with seven total points, as the deer waited beside a trail to check does heading to the fields.

The following afternoon Wayne took an extremely fine 10 point as the buck walked down a trail leading to the field. When the buck got to within about a hundred yards of the food plot he stopped and started horning a nearby bush. After he had literally destroyed it, the buck waited for the does to start coming.

Rather than shoot immediately, Wayne decided to wait and watch. Within five minutes the first does came by. The first two showed no interest at all in the buck. The third obviously was approaching her heat period. She squatted and urinated. The buck immediately took off after her, the doe leading him away from the food plot and right toward where Wayne sat in a tree stand. As the buck passed by him, Wayne squeezed the trigger of his 7 JDJ Contender handgun.

While hunting with Bill Jordan in Georgia, on Callaway Gardens in the southwestern part of the state, Bill suggested I hunt a green field where the year before I had taken a nice Southeastern buck. The first afternoon the deer started feeding in the field about an hour before dark. By the time it was too dark to see, an unbelievable number of deer were in the field -- primarily does and fawns, and a few small forkhorn bucks. The same thing occurred the second afternoon.

The third afternoon Bill and I decided I should move a ladder blind back into the trees, setting it up beside a trail -- actually where three different trails converged. We strongly suspected the larger bucks were hanging up back in the brush waiting for it to get dark. That third afternoon proved to be the charm.

Not wanting to disturb the area more than necessary,I set up the ladder blind right after lunch and immediately climbed into it. It was truly a pleasure sitting there enjoying the sights and sounds of the late October afternoon. The leaves were turning colors, and squirrels fat with acorns were leaping from tree to tree and scampering along the ground. Several times I was fooled by their noises on the ground, certain the sounds were from an approaching deer.

About three that afternoon the first deer walked by my stand and into the field, again primarily does with fawns. The first buck to pass by was a young forkhorn. He walked past my blind and headed toward a scrape, just off of the trail. He smelled of the overhanging branch, scratched the ground a couple of times, then headed toward the green field. After that several more does and fawns came by.

The next buck to appear was a decent three-year-old nine point. Immediately I was interested, but I also wanted to see what the buck would do. He walked to the scrape, nuzzled the overhanging limb, scraped the ground three times with both his left and right front feet, then urinated on his tarsal glands and let the urine trickle to the ground. His scraping duties finished he walked back toward where three trails converged and waited, staring toward the field. Shortly, a doe came by. The buck grunted a couple of times and started moving toward her with his head held low, grunting with each step he took. As he did I squeezed the trigger on my .309 JDJ Contender handgun.

Hunting food plots in late season

Hunting late in the season is much like hunting in the early part of the season. Although bucks still are interested in does, they also have become interested eating once again. Hunting near food plots where these bucks live is an especially good idea. As their sex interest wanes, bucks may be seen in food plots at different times of the day, but again primarily in the afternoon as they enter the fields just before dark. If a cold front threatens, as so often occurs at this time of the year, bucks tend to feed in advance of it. Thus, hunting right before a cold front may prove highly successful.

Bill Jordan approaches a huge typical 12 point he shot as the buck checked on does in the field, during the peak of the rut.

Hunting cropland

Hunting agricultural areas can be extremely productive. Some of the biggest antlered and bodied deer live in and around the cornfields of central North America, whether in Canada or the United States. In some instances deer move into standing corn during the hunting season. Here mature bucks have food, water and cover -- and little reason to leave. They may stay in the standing corn until it is harvested.

Successfully taking a mature buck that lives in a corn field is no easy chore. I have tried several times but succeeded only once. In that instance I knew of the deer's presence because a farmer had seen him a couple of times while checking the readiness of his corn crop. By the time I reached the farm, the owner had harvested about two-thirds of the field, but rain bought me some time. To avoid miring his equipment in mud, the farmer had chosen to delay harvesting a few days.

I started on the downwind side of the remaining corn and ever so slowly still-hunted in a zig-zag pattern, sweeping from one side to the other of the corn "thicket." As I neared the end of the field I spotted movement ahead. The deer was moving from left to right. I hurried forward and then to the right. Moments later the buck appeared in the row where I waited. The distance was short, affording an easy shot.

The author with a four-year-old Georgia buck, taken in the woods, along a trail leading to a green field.

Was I lucky in taking that buck? Without a doubt. Sometimes plans work out, other times they don't!

When standing corn, or any other tall agricultural crop has been harvested, deer simply will move to the nearest available cover. In one instance, while hunting in Tennessee, the area we planned to hunt was a series of cornfields, divided by only a couple of small creek bottoms and overgrown drainage ditches. When I arrived, the field already had been harvested. However, a significant amount of corn lay on the ground, so the deer still had an attractive food source. My host suggested I hunt in a tree along one of the narrow overgrown creek bottoms, near where a drainage ditch emptied into the creek.

The author with a big multi-tined buck taken in a food plot, on lightly hunted property.

The following evening I watched as a buck stood up in the drainage ditch. About 400 yards lay between us, too much for the .50 caliber MK-85 Modern Muzzle Loader rifle I was carrying. He stretched, then spent about five minutes looking around and hardly moving. Finally convinced there was no danger, he started slowly walking in my direction, stopping occasionally to sniff the breeze and stare at any movement. Through my binocular I could see the buck was a good 10 point with massive beams. He kept coming.

The range had decreased to about 200 yards when up popped a doe, right in front of him. She began running into the freshly harvested field, the buck right behind her. Next thing I knew, both were gone. That's how it goes sometimes when hunting mature bucks. Had I been hunting with one of my Contender handguns or a rifle I easily could have shot the buck. However only muzzle-loading rifles were legal during this particular hunting season. Such is hunting for mature deer!

Chapter 16

Hunting The Nocturnal Buck

The buck moved through the spotlight's beam, stopped momentarily to stare at me from the edge of the food plot, then disappeared into the woods. A few minutes later I spotted another monstrous buck, this one even wider, taller and with more points than the first. How I wished it were daytime instead of late at night.

The property on which these bucks lived was hunted only occasionally, and then only for does. Bucks were off limits. Obviously, the two bucks had not turned nocturnal because of hunting pressure. Nonetheless, since they had matured the only time I ever saw these bucks was between the hours of midnight and 3:00 a.m.

Three ranches away was an intensively managed property where several bucks lived. Some of the best bucks on this ranch also were nocturnal, but this second ranch was intensively managed, so many does and inferior bucks were taken each year. Only the best bucks in each age class were allowed to survive -- even if they could be found during daylight hours during the hunting season.

In evaluating these two operations, it became apparent that some bucks are primarily nocturnal regardless of the amount -- or lack -- of intense hunting pressure. In almost any deer herd some bucks become partially, if not completely, nocturnal.

On the second ranch there lived an older buck that never developed more than six total points each season throughout his life. In the antler department he was not much, but he obviously was a dominant buck in the area, because he left many offspring that looked just like him. I therefore tried hard to get rid of him, but the only time I could find him was at night. Once I had located him, I returned to the same area at first light and hunted him all morning long.

Was that taking unfair advantage of the buck? Read on.

I tried everything: baiting, rattling, scents, calls, even deer drives. Try as we might the buck evaded our every move. Even though he had unimpressive antlers, he seemed smarter than most any big antlered buck I ever had seen. The buck seemed to know what I was going to do, even before I did. To me he was the ultimate nocturnal buck.

Taking that buck required three years. When I finally did take him, it was after I had crawled into a dense thicket near where I occasionally saw him running across the road at night. I reached the thicket long before daylight and crawled into the middle of it, found a comfortable place to sit down, and waited. Just before the day was light enough for me to put features on globs of movement, I heard a deer walking on dried leaves and then bedding upwind of my hiding place. Almost immediately I could smell the musky odor of a buck.

First light came and went. So did mid-morning. My legs were beginning to cramp and the muscles in my back were screaming. But I remained still, afraid any movement would betray my presence. I had hunted and worked hard and long for a chance at the six point, if indeed this was the buck bedded in the oak brush just a few yards away.

At midday, as the sun moved straight overhead, I noticed some movement where I suspected the buck had bedded. As he stirred I

Hunting during the middle of the day is an excellent way to take a big mature buck.

got a good look at the buck's head, facing toward his backtrail. It was the six point. As he rose from his bed, I raised my rifle and squeezed the trigger. Taking that buck was as sweet and rewarding as if I had taken a record book buck.

Creatures of the night

Several of the bucks that turned nocturnal on the ranches I managed were easily identifiable, because of ear tags or freeze-brands applied when they were fawns (which turned the hair of the branded area white). These marks made recording and plotting their movements much easier, whether during the day or night. After "working" with these deer for several years I learned much about individual deer and when they moved.

The ones that fascinated me were those deer that, either from early years or as they matured, became primarily nocturnal in their movements. At the time, I used the area mostly as a research area, while the owner, his family and a few guests, as well as employees of the ranch, did nearly all of the actual hunting. They hunted by every legal method, but the harvest comprised mostly does and inferior bucks. Only a couple of good bucks were taken each year. Yet, each year, the ranch produced some extremely good bucks. The only time they were seen, however, was at night. The only hard proof we found of their existence was an occasional set of cast antlers.

On each of the ranches I manage, any number of bucks travel and move almost entirely at night. That is primarily the only time we see them. If such nocturnal bucks exist on those properties there is little doubt they exist elsewhere.

In my contacts with hunters, managers, biologists, and game wardens, every one with whom I've discussed nocturnal bucks has seen evidence of these animals. However, none of those people had concluded whether or not this behavior is an adaptation to hunting and human disturbances, or simply the time these particular deer move. Some of the deer they reported may have been poached or jack-lighted, but hardly any were taken by hunters.

Some of the nocturnal bucks live in close proximity to human habitations and even close to towns. Their presence may never be known until they are accidently killed on the highway by a motorist, or die from some other unromantic cause.

Understanding nocturnal movement

To better understand nocturnal bucks perhaps it may help to look at deer movement at night and how that affects their movement during the daytime. Considerable research, for instance, has been done on deer movement in relationship to moon phases.

The influence of the night and the moon on deer movement depends, to some extent, on whom you ask about the subject or who has conducted research in those areas. In a study conducted by *Deer & Deer Hunting* magazine in the late 1970s, readers from throughout North America supplied great amounts of data. Editor Al Hofacker compiled the information, then plotted various graphs from the information provided. He concluded, "The effect of the lunar cycle on deer activity based on this study is so minimal that it can probably be ignored as a variable that affects deer activities."

Dr. James Kroll of Texas has taken an opposing stance. Quoted by Richard P. Smith in *Deer & Deer Hunting* (January 1994), Kroll asserts, "Two of the most important influences on deer movement are temperature and moon phase, with moon phases ranking second in importance. Barometric pressure is No. 3."

In that same article, Dr. Robert Sheppard, a dedicated deer hunter and meticulous record-keeper who maintained data on three lodges in Alabama, is quoted saying, "The number of deer sighted per hunter day was 5.0 for the full moon, 3.7 for the new moon, 3.7 for the first quarter, and 3.6 for the last quarter." However when he compared the moon phases to actual kills, the last quarter ranked highest, followed by new moon, then full moon and then the first quarter.

David Morris, one of the best hunters of big mature deer, as well as one of the most knowledgeable deer experts in North America, states in his book, *Hunting Trophy Whitetails*, that during a full moon deer are more active at midday than early or late. This view coincides with what I have seen during many years of observation.

Prominent writer and astute deer observer, John Wootters of Texas, has maintained extensive records for several years. Wootters states that, because of how his data was recorded, "I can't prove it, but I suspect that whitetails move around more during the hours of 11:00 a.m. to 2:00 p.m. on days following full-moon nights."

Smith, in the article mentioned earlier, also reported on data gathered by Lynn Ketner in Georgia, Tennessee and Alabama and summarized in *Buckmaster's* magazine. Ketner reported seeing a higher percentage of bucks during the full-moon phase than any other lunar phase, and seeing the smallest percentage of bucks during the new moon phase.

It seems that, while deer have several characteristics in common, deer in different areas of the country also are different in many ways. In some areas they move with varying degrees under different moon phases. In other areas it seems that moon phases have little effect on deer movement.

So what do lunar phases have to do with nocturnal bucks? I have spent many entire nights watching deer's reactions to the lunar phases, and have noticed that when the moon is full and visible all night long, deer are not very active. They tend to lie down when the full moon rises. When the moon is dark, they also tend to lie down much of the night, but are much more active than on a full moon night. The most nocturnal activity I have seen, normally occurred the first hour after sundown, regardless of the moon's phase, or time it rose and went down. There also was a flurry activity just before first light. The nocturnal bucks I kept tabs on were most active from about midnight until about 2:00 a.m., sometimes a little later.

Nocturnal bucks at midday

During many years of hunting whitetails (especially in the Southwest, in areas such as south Texas and Mexico) and working as a biologist in the same areas, the biggest deer I have seen and taken were observed between the hours of approximately 10:30 a.m. and 3:00 p.m. During those hours I did not see nearly as many deer as I did early or late, but when a deer was seen it was generally a good, mature buck.

The author with a mature buck taken at nearly high noon.

Big bucks tended to be particularly active during these hours after an all-night full moon. They also were noticeably active during the midday after a night when there was essentially no moon. I found that the nocturnal marked bucks I was following were also most active during the middle of the day. As a matter of fact, that was the only time they ever were seen during daylight hours.

The biggest typical buck I ever have taken was shot at 11:35 a.m. after a full moon night, as the rut was beginning to wane. I started the morning by trying to rattle up bucks, which I did successfully. Both were good mature deer, but I was looking for something special. I also spent a fair amount of time still-hunting along the edge of a dry creek bottom, where previously I had seen some big bucks in the past.

About 10:30 in the morning I started working my way back to camp. Several old friends were to arrive during the mid-morning, and I was looking forward to getting together so we could get back to hunting. Back at the camp I learned they had been delayed.

I decided to head toward the back side of the property where, the year before, I had rattled up an almost 25-inch wide nine point (at high noon). Had the buck looked to be at least five years of age, I would have taken him, but by his body and facial features the buck did not look a day over three years of age -- and no more than four. Watching him walk away I had doubted my decision.

Until this day I had not yet taken a buck with a rack wider than 23 inches. Therefore it was that buck I had passed up the year previous that I now hoped to find.

As I drove toward the back part of the pasture, I remembered a buck the foreman had told me about. According to him the buck was extremely wide and tall. He had seen the buck run across the pasture road a couple of times late at night when they were shipping cattle. I decided to swing by the area where he had seen the buck. Possibly I would do some rattling or maybe a little still hunting, and if I could not find him, I would head further south.

Close to where the foreman reported having seen the deer, I spotted a group of several does feeding on a distant low hillside. As I watched I picked up the profile of a long-tined buck. He looked good, with a long main beam, two fighting tines about 12 inches long, and had what appeared to be fairly long brows -- especially for the area. Both sides appeared to be equal in size. After an embarrassing problem of trying to get my rifle out of the Jeep Cherokee I drove at the time, I grabbed my .309 JDJ Contender and took off toward where the buck was standing in the scattered brush.

The author with his largest typical whitetail taken during the middle of the day, after a full-moon night. Supposedly the buck was primarily nocturnal.

As I made my approach the does started moving off. When the buck trailed after them, I noticed how wide he actually was. I increased my pace and eventually caught up with him. When I cut the distance to about 150 yards, I found a dead tree trunk where I could get a rock-solid rest. I really needed a rest because of my shaking caused by exertion -- but mostly by excitement. When the cross-hairs settled on the target I squeezed the trigger. The deer went down immediately.

To me the sign of a big deer, after he is down, is that his antlers seem to grow, rather than shrink, as you approach. Such was the case with this buck. The closer I got, the bigger his rack seemed to get.

Kneeling at his side I whispered a prayer of thanks, hardly believing how large and wide the buck's antlers were. He had a 26-inch spread, 26-inch main beams, long primary tines, and five-inch circumference measurements. He gross scored in the mid-160s on the Boone & Crockett system. I could not have been more pleased.

That night around camp, when the other hunters arrived, there was much merriment. Throughout the night I got up several times and went out to admire the deer -- and perhaps to be sure he was real.

In the morning one of the Mexican cowboys who helped take care of the cattle on the ranch looked at the deer, then came over and shook my hand. "Señor Colorado (pronounced callarou, meaning red in Spanish), you have done well. You have taken the *macho grande del noche* (the buck of the night)!" He then explained that he had seen the buck several times before, but primarily after dark, though once at a remote waterhole during the middle of the day.

Based on my own hunting experiences, I believe nocturnal bucks are vulnerable. And, the best way to hunt them is during the middle of the day where they live. Sometimes you'll be successful, but most often you won't. In many ways they are some of the most challenging of the mature bucks. When you finally do take one of their kind, it is time for celebration, for you will have truly earned him.

Thankfully, there is an occasional "easy" one, such as the wide eight point. But even though it might have sounded easy, many, many hours of hunting had gone into the taking of that deer.

Young bucks are much more likely to expose themselves than big mature whitetails.

Chapter 17

Being Different

There are, without a doubt, many ways to hunt mature white-tailed bucks. I have tried a considerable number of tactics, some with success and others without. Some have been described in the previous chapters.

The learning never stops

Old cliches such as, "If it ain't broke, don't fix it," or "You can't teach an old dog new tricks," obviously were not aimed at hunters of mature deer. Hunting bucks that have survived several hunting seasons, as well as the sometimes even more dangerous times between seasons, is a learning experience. No matter how much you know about deer or think you know about deer, just about the time you've become convinced you know what they will do, they will teach you another new trick or two.

I am constantly trying to learn from the mistakes of others and, unfortunately, my own. By listening and watching I learn much about deer. In addition, I have been fortunate to have hunted with some of the best whitetail hunters who ever have pulled on a pair of camouflaged or wool britches.

Fellow biologist Steve Warner taught me a trick or two about using bicycles to get into hunting areas, thus leaving no scent trail. Using his handlebar transportation, Steve cycled into an area frequented by a double drop-tine buck. He set up near a pond that had flooded several weeks earlier and then subsided, creating a carpet of lush forb growth. When the buck came to feed on the highly palatable weeds, Warner shot him. All other attempts at the buck had been thwarted, primarily because the buck would circle the area until he picked up the scent of a human walking into the area, or at least so it seemed. Warner has since taken his mountain bike on the road, to use it when hunting deer in other areas.

Bob Parker, Jr. taught me a lesson about watching armadillos in south Texas. Bob noticed that when armadillos were active, so were the deer. My dad and grandad had taught me to watch what cattle do and suggested there was a positive correlation, that deer and other animals moved and fed at approximately the same times. Since that time I have gone back to watching cattle and armadillos, as well as squirrels.

Steve Warner with his handlebars buck.

No justice

Mature deer sometimes show up in the darndest places, especially in areas where they are not expected, such as at the front yard of a hunting camp or lodge. On one of the ranches I managed the owner allowed only guests and clients to hunt. Most who were invited were not particularly serious hunters. They, instead, came down to have a good time.

We did allow the consumption of alcohol, but only after dark. Drinking any alcohol during the day was forbidden and was grounds for being asked to leave and not come back. If someone drank a fair amount at night, he was not allowed to hunt the next morning. I was the one who made those arbitrary decisions.

190

One night a guest imbibed a little too much. Thus, the next morning he was not allowed to go into the field. By the expression on his face he was not too disappointed. About 9:00 a.m. I heard a shot from the direction of camp. Naturally I was concerned so I headed back in a hurry. When I reached the front yard of the camp, there stood the non-hunting guest, wearing cowboy boots, his boxer shorts and an old hat. At his feet lay a 22-inch 10 point buck with several nontypical points, a deer I never had seen on the property. I asked for an explanation.

When the guest had risen to answer the call of nature, he happened to peer out the window to see how light it was. Instead, he noticed the buck feeding on rose bushes in the front yard. Though his coordination was not yet reliable, he managed to find his rifle, locate his shells, load one cartridge into the rifle and shoot the deer, which died on the spot. After I approached the hunter, he handed me the rifle and staggered back to bed. He was not our typical hunter, neither in his behavior and manner, nor in terms of the deer he took.

There sometimes seems to be no justice in who takes the best and biggest deer. No one wanted to hunt close to camp or from the front porch, even though I had seen several good deer from the front porch swing. Everyone in such a camp wants to hunt the far ends of the property. Therefore, being different normally pays off.

Many of the veteran south Texas ranchers I know are proponents of hunting from about 9:00 a.m. till about noon. They rise early, long before daylight, to get their hunters to their hunting areas, drink coffee for couple of hours, lie back down for an extended nap, then get up about 9:00 and go hunting -- just about the time the hunters on the ranch are heading back to camp. By noon the old rancher is back with a big deer, and he is accused of having a buck staked out and knowing exactly where he is.

There may be some truth in the accusation, because the rancher has spent considerable time on the property and knows the lay of the land. But he also knows some of the bigger bucks may not move until mid-morning or midday. Being different sometimes may be the best way to hunt, especially if you are looking to take a mature deer.

Hunting in a hay bale

Several years ago a friend of mine in the Southeast started seeing a particularly large buck for his area in the middle of a huge hay field. Evidently the buck moved into the field before daylight, remained there all day long, then headed to the woods during the cover of darkness -- and returned before first light. The field was wide open except for a scattering of big round hay bales. My friend tried several times to put the sneak on the buck, but always was detected long before he drew within 500 yards of the buck.

The hunter thought of several options, from digging a pit in the middle of the field to procuring a rifle capable of 700-yard shots. However, he began noticing the buck seemed to pay little attention to the large round hay bales, and several times approached within 200 yards of them. This hatched a plan.

My friend built his own "bale" out of mesh wire and hay and straw. The wire cage, was about 7 feet in diameter and about 7 feet tall. Between the strands of wire he wove straw and hay, producing what looked just like the other hay bales in the field.

That night he placed the bogus hay bale in the middle of the 300-acre field. The next morning, before daylight, he was in his blind. At first light he spotted the buck lying about 400 yards away.

While the buck looked the other way, the hunter started rolling the hay bale by walking inside it as if in a treadmill. Through holes he occasionally could see the buck. Whenever the buck appeared about to look his way, the hunter stopped. When the buck looked away again the hunter resumed rolling toward the deer.

After a while the buck got up and started feeding. When the deer's head was down the hunter rolled the hay bale blind forward. When the deer looked up the hunter stopped. After about a half hour, the man had moved to within about 200 yards of the buck. Using the wire mesh as a rest, he squeezed a shot at the deer. It fell immediately.

Regardless of how you hunt and what techniques you use, basics such as keeping the sun at your back, and the wind in your face should never be overlooked.

The hunter's attempt at being different proved worthwhile. He has since used his hay bale blind numerous times to take good deer, not only in the Southeast, but in the flat country of Wyoming, south Texas, and Montana as well.

Deer hunting is for dummies

Sometime ago I found a good buck that frequented a huge wheat field. The owner of the property had set up a permanent tall tower near the spot where the buck usually crossed under the fence. However, if someone sat in the tower the buck would move to the other end of the mile-long field. But if no one was in the tower blind, he crossed into the field within 100 yards of it. Apparently the buck had observed and studied the tower blind until he could determine whether or not a hunter was in it. This knowledge helped him decide where he would enter the field. I decided we should place a mannequin in the tower to see what the buck would do.

That night we built a dummy deer hunter. Several in camp insisted the dummy was a spitting image of this writer/biologist, not only in outward appearance, but in deer hunting knowledge as well. I just smiled. The next day we set the mannequin in the tower.

The following night the buck crossed into the field near its end. We left the dummy in the blind for several days, giving the buck plenty of opportunity to become familiar with the dummy hunter in the tower blind. After about two weeks of this, we decided to see what would happen if the tower was occupied by a live hunter. The hunter sat perfectly still and wore clothing similar to that worn by the dummy.

That afternoon one of the ranch's paying hunters climbed into the tower blind. About an hour before dark we heard a shot and returned to retrieve the hunter -- and hopefully the big buck. We found the buck lying fewer than 100 yards from the blind, just beyond the barbed wire fence where he had crossed into the wheat field. The dummy had done the trick!

On another occasion a dummy deer hunter also did the trick for me -- but in a different manner. Several times I had seen a nice, mature buck cross a logging road that separated two planted sections of pine. A ground blind was out of the question because its location would not allow me to see the area where he crossed, or would be too close to the crossing. Thus, I set up a tripod where I could see the narrow road. That afternoon the deer crossed just beyond range. He had peered out of the wall of pines, seen the tripod, then moved further down the road to cross.

The next afternoon as I headed to the woods, I took a mannequin dressed in hunting clothes and sat it in the tripod. With the dummy hunter in place I moved down the road, not far where the buck had crossed the road on his way to a nighttime feeding area the afternoon before.

About an hour before dark the buck's head appeared on the road between the tripod and me. He looked toward the tripod, then withdrew and disappeared. Just shy of 10 minutes later, the buck reappeared, this time not 30 steps from where I sat hidden in the grass and pines. That night, when I arrived in camp with a good buck and my new deer hunting "partner," there was not near as much laughing about a dummy as there had been when I left earlier!

In praise of smelly socks

Much has been written about how deer avoid areas that have an abundance of human scents. On several occasions, by using sources of human odor, I have caused deer to shift their movement to areas I wanted them to travel. Sweat-soaked shirts or even smelly socks hung along trails "persuaded" those deer to take an alternate route.

On a ranch I managed for several years, one 20-acre high-fenced pasture was home to no less than 20 to 30 bucks, as well as an equal number of does and fawns. The deer were fed a high-protein ration, free choice, so they had plenty to eat. This pen, if you wish to call it that, held numerous large-antlered mature bucks that were photographed by an old friend, Judd Cooney.

In time the deer learned to avoid and counteract our every move as we tried to drive them by Judd's camera. That's when we started hanging dirty laundry along certain trails in an attempt to encourage them toward particular trails where they could be photographed. It worked to perfection. Later we started doing the same thing when hunting. Remember my emphasis on odor-free hunting? If you look hard enough there almost always are ways to turn negatives into positives.

Dare to be REALLY different

Perhaps such is the case with an elderly man who lives near my home. I often had marveled at the huge whitetail racks mounted in his home and hunting camp. He had started hunting whitetails in Mexico, Canada, and his native Texas long before hunting for big-racked whitetails became the thing to do. Naturally, we occasionally talked about hunting big deer.

Even though he no longer hunted in other states he still hunted his personal ranch in the brush country of south Texas. I knew the ranch held some big bucks, but I always was amazed at the consistency with which he took good deer.

One night, while sitting around a mesquite campfire recalling great deer we had hunted, we began talking about some of the unique things we had done to take mature bucks. It was then he confided one of his secrets, even though he often had told me he was a confirmed scrape hunter.

"I've never told anyone this, mainly because most hunters probably would have told me I was nuts. But, for years I have been hunting scrapes, especially in areas where the previous winter I found

Mature bucks are huge of body!

big shed horns, or happened to see deer while we were working cattle on horseback. As the rut was about to get started and bucks were scraping in earnest, I'd start visiting them and freshening them myself, urinating in them every time I went by a scrape. It drove the bucks mad. Took that 23 point nontypical hanging behind my desk in that way."

He hesitated, then poked at the coals, sending a spray of bright orange sparks skyward. He took a sip of branch water and continued, "One of the old Mexican *vaqueros* who used to work for my dad taught me the trick. When he first told me, I laughed at him. But then I started paying attention to him when he started shooting a monstrous buck each fall with an old, open-sighted .44-40 saddle gun.

"According to the *brasada de veijo* (old man of the brush), his urinating in the buck's scrape made the deer check his scrape more frequently. After that I started doing the same. I began taking some really good bucks, better bucks than what I shot any other way. I have used the trick from Canada to Mexico."

I found his comments interesting, for they certainly were different from anything I had heard for years. However, recent research has shown there is little, if any, difference between urines of different animals -- even humans.

All this sound odd? Perhaps in some ways it is. But then, sometimes to take the buck of your dreams you need to dare to be different.

Chapter 18

The Supreme Challenge: Over-the-Hill Bucks

Over many years it has been my extreme pleasure to have hunted several old bucks -- old in age and wisdom. If hunting mature bucks that move primarily at night is challenging, then perhaps the supreme challenge in the whitetail hunting world is hunting the over-the-hill bucks.

Age and antler development

In an earlier chapter I mentioned that some bucks produce just enough testosterone to go through the antler development cycle, but not really enough to be sexually active, even during the peak of the rut. Some over-the-hill bucks might just fit into this category, but not necessarily all of them. I have observed some bucks remaining sexually active until they were 14 years old.

Just because a buck supposedly is past his peak in antler development does not mean he has unimpressive antlers. I have seen several bucks that grew bigger antlers every year, no matter how old they were, as long as they received a high-energy, high-protein diet, well-balanced in minerals and vitamins. One of the best bucks I have encountered was a deer that, when 13 years old, grew the best rack of his life. That year his rack netted 242 Boone & Crockett points.

In the case of another deer, we found shed antlers from a particular buck that lived to be 11 years of age. The year he was shot, his gross score was in the 180s. As a four-year-old he would have scored only in the 140s. Throughout his life, starting with his third year, his back tine was deeply forked. He maintained that same antler style throughout his life and was readily identifiable -- or at least his sheds were.

Several of the bucks I have kept tabs on over the years had their best antlers when eight or nine years old. Because few deer in the wilds ever get to live that long, we do not know if these were exceptions rather than the rule.

Nonetheless, while not all bucks produce their best antlers at this advanced age and beyond, I find that this is when bucks have their most interesting antlers. They may add non-typical or "kicker" points. Their normally round beams and tines might start showing some angularity. To me the racks produced by these over-the-hill bucks show much "character."

In my book a buck gains the title of over-the-hill when he surpasses his seventh year. That's an extremely old deer in many areas, simply because of hunting pressure, predation, and the perils of nature. Those that do survive become masters of evasion, so hunting them truly becomes a supreme challenge. Sometimes those challenges are successful and sometimes not!

Wily old bucks and a hunter's persistence

On the wall of my office hang no fewer than 20 mounted white-tailed deer shoulder mounts, while several others hang at my old hunting camp near my childhood home. All except one spike, my first buck, are mounts of mature deer. Even though some of the racks are larger, my favorite deer are those for which I hunted several years. Those include a buck displaying three drop-tines on one side with a total of 18 points and a 22-inch spread.

I hunted that buck for seven years, during which I saw him only twice. The first time I saw him, he was a mature deer. He had about a 26-inch spread with 10 long points, several kicker points, about an 8-inch drop-tine on left side, and about a 3-inch drop on the right side. Unfortunately, the beginning of the hunting season was a full month away.

Each fall I hunted the buck whenever I had opportunity. Yet, regardless of what I did, the buck evaded me time and again. I knew the deer was still alive because he was seen, although rarely, by one of the workers on the property. When I finally did take the buck, I shot him near the end of the season, near the spot where I first had seen him several years earlier.

I never have hunted as hard or as long for a deer as I did for that one. Taking that old buck, therefore, certainly has been a highlight of my hunting career. I have told the story of the old buck many different times, around campfires and in print.

Another deer I hunted for a long time was a double drop-tine buck. He was one of the few such bucks I have seen, although I have seen thousands of bucks while hunting and doing game surveys. I started hunting the deer the year I first saw him, when he showed up only about 200 hundred yards from the hunting lodge. (The deer season still was well over a month away, and I was getting the lodge in order for the upcoming season.) At that time he had eight long points with the double drops, both about 5 or 6 inches long.

Throughout the hunting season I hunted the buck, as did three other hunters. Yet we never saw the buck during that season. The following fall I again saw the buck not far from where we had seen him the year before, so again several of us hunted for him. But no one saw him. Trying to determine where the deer was going during the hunting season occupied a lot of discussion around that hunting camp each fall.

The author approaches the long-tined buck he hunted for several years. The buck's sheds lead to his undoing.

Then I learned the buck had appeared nearby on adjoining property that was closed to any hunting. One day, while I was visiting with the neighbor's cattle foreman, he mentioned having seen a good double drop-tine buck on one of their fields about 2 miles east of our headquarters. The only time he saw the buck was during the hunting season. The buck would stay in near the field throughout the rut, then disappear again until the following November. The foreman said the deer was quite a buck. Unfortunately he did not offer to invite me to come hunt the buck on their property.

A couple of years later, when on the property, I had shifted to hunting for a long-tined 10 point whose shed antlers I had found. Then one day, right near the end of the season, Ron Porter, a long-time hunting partner, and I were hunting the area near where I originally had seen the drop-tine buck. Suddenly a tall basic eight point buck stepped out, a long distance away. Peering through a spotting scope, Ron announced the buck had a couple of short drop tines, one on each side.

Immediately we planned a stalk. When we got to within about 200 yards the buck started running. I shot at him twice. Both shots missed. With that the buck was gone, and I was convinced I had missed my chance at the buck, forever!

The next morning as I walked from one area to another, I spotted a buck walking toward me along the edge of a huge over-grown field. I dropped to a sitting position and quickly set up my crossed shooting sticks to get a solid rest. The buck walked to within about a hundred yards of me. The shot was almost anti-climatic. But when it sounded, I had claimed an old buck that had eluded me for several years.

A third over-the-hill buck whose mount hangs in my office is the deer I switched to when it appeared I would have no opportunity to take the double drop-tine buck just described. Ron Porter and I had found the buck's shed antlers. Most impressive were the rack's 28-inch main beams and 14-inch primary tines. Giving the buck an in-side spread of 18 inches, it easily would have met the record book minimum for typicals.

The following fall I started hunting the buck. And for the next three years I hunted him whenever I was in that part of the country. I saw the buck before the season, after the season, and occasionally during the season -- unfortunately only after dark, while I was working on the property. Each time I saw him during the season at night he was near the spot where we had found the shed antlers. And each time I saw him before or after the season he was in the same area. But those original sheds were the only shed antlers I ever found from the buck.

During those years I tried rattling, hunting scrapes, still-hunting, watching nearby feeding areas -- everything but deer drives. The year I finally shot the buck, I had traveled to the lodge to pre-pare it for what was being forecast as one of the year's worst winter storms. After preparing the lodge and making sure the livestock would have sufficient hay during the coming ice storm, I decided to make one last trip through the pastures before heading to another operation to the same preparations.

As I drove down a pasture road I spotted a deer that looked like a buck, and a good one at that. I quickly parked my Suburban and walked in the direction of the deer. Using every bit of available cover

I was able to stalk to within 200 yards of deer. Through my binocular I noticed the buck's tines were extremely tall, although he was relatively narrow. And there was something familiar about his antlers, especially the long tines. Then I realized they looked somewhat like the sheds we had found some time earlier. That was all I needed to swap my binocular for my rifle. When the cross-hairs settled on the deer's shoulder I squeezed the trigger on my .280 Remington. The buck dropped.

The closer I got to the downed deer the more his tines seemed to lengthen. Four of the tines measured over 11 inches long, two of which were over 13 inches in length. The main beams were both in excess of 26 inches. The buck's teeth were worn down to his gumline, making him easily over eight years old. There was little doubt this was the buck I had been hunting since finding his shed antlers several years earlier. Although his rack was impressive, it did not quite measure up to what it once had been. Nonetheless I knew I had taken a buck that once had been a record book deer!

Weishuhn with an old, over-the-hill buck, taken after hunting him for several years.

If there was one thing that led to the taking of those three deer it was simply that I was persistent. Persistence is often a key factor in taking big bucks. But so is plain old good luck, even though I generally describe the term "luck" as that point in time when knowledge and opportunity meet. Regardless of the definition "luck" played an important part in the taking of the three bucks I mentioned.

Not so lucky

Other times I have not been so lucky. On one of the places I hunted for a couple of years I was told of a big 10 point buck that lived near a thicket next to a flowing creek. During a late summer scouting trip I made my way through the bottom country next to the creek. I was wearing snake leggings and paying particular attention to the possibility of running into a cottonmouth moccasin, a thought I did not relish! As I tiptoed through the willows, perspira-

201

tion was falling freely from my forehead onto my glasses. Between the two distractions of snakes and sweat, I was paying little attention to what was ahead of me. That is how I nearly stepped on the buck.

When the buck spooked he did so in a hurry. All I really got to see of him as he jumped into more cover was his rack. That brief glimpse convinced me he would be worth hunting when I returned to the property in January. Before flying home I recorded various data in my buck journal and made notes on the map of the property. I hoped the buck would survive until January.

When late January finally arrived, I made my way to the creek bottom where I had jumped the buck the previous July. Though unsure the buck would still be there, I was willing to take a chance he was. I still-hunted my way to the edge of the creek, to a large rock from where I could see a good portion of the creek bottom. Shortly after arriving I decided to try rattling, even though I strongly suspected the season was too late for attracting a buck with my horns.

I started tickling the horns, imitating a late post-rut fight. No sooner had I started than the buck I was hunting burst out of the brush beneath me. Swiftly I pointed the .375 Winchester Thompson/Center Contender in the direction of the buck. Finding the deer in my Simmons scope I squeezed the trigger. To my amazement the buck ran off, and before I could reload he was gone. It took a while for me to realize and accept I had missed! That was the last I saw of the deer that year.

The following July I returned to the same hollow and again scouted the area. While there I picked up a shed antler of the deer I had seen the year previous. The shed indicated the buck was past his prime and heading down hill, based on comparison of the pedicel attachment to the circumference of the beam just above the burr. I became even more interested in returning to hunt the old buck. Unfortunately, I could not return to the property before late January.

When I finally got back to the property the landlord had planted a corn field next to the creek, creating an ideal place for big bucks, with food, water and cover. Based on where I had seen the buck in the past, I decided to get in the middle of the flowing stream and ease along slowly with the northwesterly breeze blowing in my face. After putting on a pair of over-the-boots waders, I took my time moving through the water. When I was even with the still standing cornfield, I moved into it.

As I entered the field, a ruckus arose behind me. I turned in time to see a big-bodied doe take off running through the corn. Just then another deer ran off in the opposite direction. It sounded as if a herd of cattle was running, knocking down corn stalks as they did.

I caught a glimpse of a buck that looked very much like the one I had missed the year before. But, before I could get my rifle in position for a shot, he was gone. Again.

I hunted the area for the next three days, saw some young bucks that needed a couple more years before they would be mature, but never saw the old, over-the-hill buck.

Does the story end there? Surely I hope not. Actually I hope there always will be an over-the-hill white-tailed buck to hunt somewhere!

Chapter 19

Trials and Tales of Mature Bucks

Each of us is looking for the easy way to take a big, mature white-tail. We buy a great variety of products and gadgets, thinking they will give us that extra little edge. But, the truth is, we need to be careful not to overlook the basics. In other words, principles such as keeping the wind in our face when hunting -- except when rattling; keeping the sun at our back; remembering always to move slowly when we are in the woods; and never to drop our guard -- because as soon as we do the mature buck will take advantage of that weakness.

Overlooking or forgetting basics such as knowing your firearm's or bow's, and (maybe more importantly) your own capabilities, can make the difference between taking home a good deer or reliving that miss again and again in the future. I have experienced both, especially far more misses than I sometimes care to admit.

I admit to shooting at and missing two Boone & Crockett white-tails, one in Canada and one in Mexico. I also have missed a couple of bucks while appearing on national television. Then there was the buck I missed in north Texas by shooting through a mesquite limb. That afternoon, baseball great Nolan Ryan took the buck I had missed. The buck grossed in the high 160s on the Boone & Crockett system. And there have been several others.

In most instances, analysis of why I missed a shot, or why I missed opportunities at bucks, has shown that the basics had been neglected. And I have relived those misses again and again. But, hopefully, I have learned from my mistakes.

The lessons of experience

Mature whitetails have taught me many lessons, not only about deer and hunting, but occasionally even about myself. Mature bucks can, at times, be completely unpredictable, and yet, at other times, can be almost embarrassingly easy -- even when they should not be. Such was the case with a big 11 point I took while doing a television show for ESPN's *North American Outdoors*.

I was hunting for a couple of days on the Perlitz Ranch near Crystal City, Texas, with Bill Whitfield and Bill Miller, the host of the show. By the time I arrived at the ranch the two Bills and Jimmy Perlitz had located a pair of interesting mature bucks for us to hunt. The first afternoon in camp, Bill Miller shot an interesting non-typical buck with double main beams on one side. That night we celebrated Bill's success, as well as the success of having at least one show "in the can."

Sometimes taking to the streams is a good way to find bucks. In some areas bucks tend to bed near streams, in other areas they avoid such areas.

The buck they had planned for me to hunt was a beautiful, typical 11 point buck. I had seen the buck before, while filming a show with Bill Jordan for his TNN show, *Realtree Outdoors*. Bill had missed the buck with his bow, but in the process David Blanton had recorded a lot of footage of the buck. Thus, I knew the deer was a good one.

Shortly after first light, Bill Miller and I climbed into a large permanent blind near where the buck had been seen numerous times. During our first 30 minutes we saw 15 bucks with eight or more points. Just as if on cue, when the light was good enough for filming, the typical 11 point appeared. The cameraman went to work recording the buck.

After a couple minutes of filming I got the go ahead to take the animal. I raised the .35 Remington XP-100, centered the Simmons scope on the buck's shoulder and squeezed the trigger. Dust flew up about halfway to the deer, and Bill gasped, "You missed!"

As the deer ran off, I sat in total disbelief at having missed -- on

After missing the buck on national television the author was ready to go back to camp. His guide insisted they stay. Ten minutes later the buck reappeared. Never try to outguess a mature whitetail.

a national television program. Obviously the buck was leading a charmed life. He had been missed twice while being filmed for national broadcast, first by Bill Jordan and now by me. I shook my head. Bill started laughing, then I did too. Just as well laugh as cry! I suggested go back to camp and have a cup of coffee. But since on this occasion Bill was my guide, rather than the other way around, he suggested we stay right there.

What happened next proved I always should listen to my guide. Fewer than 10 minutes after I missed the buck, the same deer walked out and stood in the road leading from the main ranch road to the blind. This time my aim was true! I suppose sometimes victory has to be snatched from the jaws of defeat, even though it seems one is doing just the opposite.

That same year I hunted with Bill Whitfield on the Encinitos Ranch near McAllen, Texas, in what used to be known as the Wild Horse Desert. Whenever Whitfield and I hunt together, things just seem to happen. The year before, Bill and I had found a tremendous typical 11 point buck with a kicker point. But rather than shoot we decided the deer was not quite mature and needed another year.

The following fall I saw the deer while doing a helicopter game survey. He indeed had improved and was now a monster, displaying a couple more kicker points, including deep forks on his back tines.

Whitfield and I, along with Bill Jordan of Realtree, baseball great Wade Boggs, and several others hunted the deer. But could not find him. However, the deer -- or so I thought -- was taken by one of Whitfield's clients. The five year old deer gross-scored in excess of 180 Boone & Crockett points. Bill was convinced it was the deer we had seen and passed, and the same one I had seen during the helicopter game survey.

Then, in February, when conducting our annual helicopter game survey, I saw a buck that looked exactly like the one that had been taken and the one I had seen the year before. Different deer? Same deer? Honestly, I am not sure. I am just happy there is another deer that big out there, and cannot wait to hunt him. The saga continues.

The Mexican giants

The arid brushy lands of Mexico are home to some monstrous whitetails. Hunting there is like taking a step back into the past. Ranches are large, and those that have been maintained well have excellent deer populations.

Jim Raney of Brush Country Guide Service, based out of McAllen, Texas, operates hunts on some of the best ranches south of the Rio Grande. I combined with Bill Jordan and former professional football standout, Steve Bartkowski, for a hunt with Raney. During that hunt I saw four of the best bucks I have seen in many years.

Stan White, who had hunted the ranch for several years, told me about a buck he had hunted in one of the expansive pastures. He described it as a big typical 12

Weishuhn with an extremely large buck that was hunted for many years before he was finally taken.

point, whose kicker points on the back tines appeared as flags flying from each tine. The first time I saw the buck he stood staring in my direction from a distance of over 1,000 yards. He stood on top of the ridge, I sat in a tripod in the bottom of the valley. The buck was monstrous!

That same morning I saw another typical 12 that appeared to easily surpass the Boone & Crockett minimum. He stood almost exact-

The author with a mature buck taken in Mexico after seeing some huge deer, which he could not get close enough to for a shot.

ly where the "flag" buck had stood. Moments later, a 10 point with about a 26- or 27-inch outside spread stood in the exact same spot.

Shortly after that buck disappeared, the most massive antlered buck I ever have seen alive appeared in the same spot, and then he too disappeared. The massive buck was unbelievable, impressing me more than the record-book bucks I had just seen. That same morning I saw numerous other good mature bucks, including an eight point with about a 25-inch spread, which I now wish I had taken.

When things slowed, I moved my tripod 1,025 yards to where I the big bucks had crossed the *sendero*. That afternoon I suggested to Stan he hunt from the tripod in hopes of taking the deer -- which

Mature bucks, with antlers spread well beyond forward, erect ears, are constantly on the alert. As a hunter you had better be the same!

he had been hunting for several days. Stan crawled into the tripod at about 2:30 p.m. At 4:00 that afternoon the buck appeared, in the very spot from which I had moved the tripod.

That night Stan and I decided we would combine on the deer. I would hunt the tripod on the ridge. He would set up a ground blind in the valley where the tripod had been previously. We were in our respective blinds well before first light

Between daylight and 9:15 a.m., I saw 20 different bucks, but not the big bucks. At 9:20 a.m. Stan left his ground blind to do his part in the television show chronicling the hunt. At 9:23 a.m. I watched in awe as the Boone & Crockett non-typical contender we were hunting walked out right behind Stan's now empty ground blind. The buck fed on fresh green growth in the recently mowed *sendero* for five minutes, often within fewer than 20 steps of Stan's blind. Finally the buck walked right by the ground blind and disappeared into the dense brush. I did not see any other big bucks that morning.

When I told Stan what had happened, he could hardly believe what the "flag" buck had done. I just considered it typical mature buck behavior -- something to which I had grown accustomed whenever hunting the super bucks. That afternoon, my last day to hunt, just before dark I shot a mature, massively antlered 10 point buck.

The big bucks we had hunted and seen? They still are there as this is being written. However, as long as the good Lord allows me that grand privilege, I will go back and do my best to hunt the "flag" buck and his kin!

Chapter 20

What of the Future? Maybe Tomorrow!

The fire in the old rock fireplace was burning low, while outside the wind was blowing hard from the north. The temperature had dropped steadily since sundown. I threw another log on the fire. As the flames warmed both body and soul, I stared at the mount of a big mature white-tailed buck above the fireplace.

He was quite a buck, representing not only many hours of hunting, but also a deer management success story. The buck had been born the year hunters on the property had initiated a quality deer management program. The growing buck had benefited from the improved and increased food supply, provided through plantings of forage crops. In addition, a reduction of the overall deer herd had insured plenty of quality forage and browse for each deer throughout the entire year.

The deer herd had benefitted greatly from the management program, but maybe not nearly as much as the many birds, including game, song and raptors; small animals such as rodents, reptiles, amphibians and others; and predators and other animals that now called the improved wildlife habitat home. Possibly more important, however, was that the plants and overall habitat were benefiting most from such a program.

Those of us who had initiated the quality management program, and helped maintain it through the difficult years, were proud of what had been accomplished. Even so, hunters everywhere should be proud of what they have done for wildlife through what is commonly called "wildlife conservation." Without the monies provided

The future of mature whitetails is looking better all the time. Full meat poles are important, but not nearly as important as enjoying the hunt and having fun!

by hunters, and especially whitetail hunters, wildlife in general would be in sad shape.

The outlook for white-tailed deer is excellent. The greatest threat whitetails face comes in the form of misinformed people who support the anti-hunting and anti-gun movements. If the death knell ever is sounded for white-tailed deer -- and most of the other wildlife in this world -- it will be because of the well-intentioned but sadly misdirected efforts of people who oppose hunting.

Hopefully, in time, common sense and scientific research will replace emotion and hysteria in the decision-making regarding what really is best for wildlife and wildlife habitat. For this I have fought hard. I have fought the good fight and will continue doing so as long as I am physically able.

My musing ceased momentarily. The mature white-tailed buck on the wall was a sign of success. I loved him dearly.

The back log was nearly gone, and the warm bed beckoned. In the coals of black and orange and their wisps of smoke I was now visualizing the many bucks I had hunted, those that had been taken, those that I wished I had taken, and those that I simply had admired. I had learned something from each of them. My gaze lingered on the flames for a few final moments.

Maybe the morrow would finally bring me face to face with THE buck, the one for which I have hunted all my life. But I secretly hoped such a buck would still be a long way into the future. For most of my life, by the grace of God, I have lived a dream and I am most certainly thankful. May there always be mature bucks to provide us with challenges in the future, both yours and mine.

Zero in on successful deer hunting with these four exciting new books!

WHITETAIL: THE ULTIMATE CHALLENGE
by Charles J. Alsheimer
6"x9", softcover, 228 pg., 150 photos
Learn deer hunting's most intriguing secrets from America's
premier authority on using decoys, scents and calls to bag a

buck. Find insight on the
whitetail's rut cycles, where and
how to hunt whitetails across
North America, rubs, scrapes,
the impact of weather conditions and much more! Plus,
many spectacular black and
white photos.

$14⁹⁵

Available June 1995

HUNTING MATURE BUCKS
by Larry Weishuhn
6"x9", softcover, 256 pg., 80 photos
Learn how to take those big, smart, elusive bucks.
Excellent blend of scientific knowledge and old-fashioned
"how-to" gives you the informa-
tion you need. Also learn
behind the scenes management
techniques that help balance
doe/buck ratios to produce
bragging-size whitetails.

Available February 1995

$14⁹⁵

AGGRESSIVE WHITETAIL HUNTING
by Greg Miller
6"x9", paperback, 208 pg., 80 photos
Learn how to hunt trophy bucks in public forests and
farmlands from one of America's foremost hunters.

"Hunter's hunter" Greg Miller
puts his years of practical
experience into easy-to-
understand advice that will help
both bow and gun hunters bag
that trophy. Ideal for busy
outdoorsmen that have neither
the time nor finances to hunt
exotic locales.

$14⁹⁵

Available February 1995

SOUTHERN DEER & DEER HUNTING
by Bill Bynum and Larry Weishuhn

These two popular southern hunters and DEER & DEER
HUNTING field editors join forces to bring you the history of
deer in the south, plus tech-
niques that work below the
Mason Dixon line as well as
anywhere whitetails are found.
Understand terrain, firearms,
equipment, rattling and calling
along with much more firsthand
experience that's guaranteed to
bring you success in southern
climates.

$14⁹⁵

Available June 1995

ORDER TODAY! BUY ALL FOUR BOOKS AND GET FREE SHIPPING!*

Please send me:

____ copy(ies) WHITETAIL: THE ULTIMATE CHALLENGE...$14.95 $ _____

____ copy(ies) HUNTING MATURE BUCKS...$14.95 $ _____

____ copy(ies) AGGRESSIVE WHITETAIL HUNTING...$14.95 $ _____

____ copy(ies) SOUTHERN DEER & DEER HUNTING...$00.00 $ _____

Shipping ($2.50 for first book, $1.50 for each
additional book, FREE if you buy all four) $ _____

WI residents add 5.5% sales tax $ _____

Total Amount Enclosed $ _____

Name _____
Address _____
City _____
State _____ Zip _____
❑ Check or money order (to Krause Publications)
❑ MasterCard ❑ VISA
Credit Card No. _____
Expires: Mo. _____ Yr. _____
Signature _____

Mail with payment to:
KRAUSE PUBLICATIONS
Book Dept. VZB2, 700 E. State St., Iola, WI 54990-0001

Books shipped upon publication

**For faster service MasterCard and VISA
customers dial toll-free**
800-258-0929 Dept. VZB2
6:30 am - 8:00 pm, Sat. 8:00 am - 2:00 pm, CT

DEER & DEER HUNTING: *A Hunter's Guide to Deer Behavior & Hunting Techniques*
Al Hofacker, Editor
Al Hofacker, founder and former editor of the popular Deer & Deer Hunting magazine, combines his outdoor experience with his editor's quill to bring you one of the finest deer hunting guides available.
$34.95, Hardcover, 8-1/2"x11", 208 pp., 100 color photos

1995 DEER HUNTERS' ALMANAC
Staff of Deer & Deer Hunting Magazine
A great way to start the season, the new 1995 edition is loaded with helpful facts, forecasts, ballistic data and hunting tips. It makes a perfect hunting companion.
$6.95, Softcover, 5-1/4"x8-1/4", 208 pp., 50+ b&w photos

301 VENISON RECIPES: *The Ultimate Deer Hunter's Cookbook*
Staff of DEER & DEER HUNTING Magazine
If you need to feed a hungry bunch at deer camp, or serve special guests in your home, look no further for creative ways to prepare hearty and delicious venison.
$10.95, Comb-bound, 6"x9", 128 pp.

ADVANCED WHITETAIL DETAILS
Staff of DEER & DEER HUNTING Magazine
This reference includes the first-ever transparent overlays of white-tailed deer anatomy! As a comprehensive yet easy-to-read handbook, it answers the technical questions most often asked by experienced deer hunters.
$14.95, Spiral-bound, 8-1/2"x11", 24 pp., 50+ photos/charts

1995 WHITETAIL CALENDAR
The seventh edition of our Whitetail Calendar contains 12 full-color photos even more stunning than those featured in previous years. The DEER & DEER HUNTING Whitetail Calendar is perfect for home, office or your hunting cabin.
$7.95, Unfolds to 2-1/8"x16-3/4"